AF333240

Howard Mumford Jones

and the Dynamics of Liberal Humanism

Howard Mumford Jones

and the Dynamics of Liberal Humanism

Peter Brier

UNIVERSITY OF MISSOURI PRESS COLUMBIA AND LONDON

University of Missouri Press, Columbia, Missouri 65201
Printed and bound in the United States of America

5 4 3 2 1 98 97 96 95 94

Library of Congress Cataloging-in-Publication Data

Brier, Peter A.
Howard Mumford Jones and the dynamics of liberal humanism / Peter Brier.
p. cm.
Includes bibliographical references (p.) and index.
ISBN 0-8262-0944-0 (alk. paper)
1. Jones, Howard Mumford, 1892–1980. 2. American literature—History and criticism—Theory, etc. 3. Liberalism—United States—History—20th century. 4. Humanism—United States—History—20th century. I. Title.
PS3519.0425Z55 1994
809—dc20 93-47306
CIP

⊗™ This paper meets the requirements of the American National Standard for Permanence of Paper for Printed Library Materials, Z39.48, 1984.

Designer: Kristie Lee
Typesetter: Connell-Zeko Type & Graphics
Printer and binder: Thomson-Shore, Inc.
Typeface: Palatino

Title page illustration from Howard Mumford Jones, *Howard Mumford Jones: An Autobiography* (Madison: University of Wisconsin Press, 1979).

In memory of my father

Francis Simon Brier

BORN, VIENNA, AUSTRIA-HUNGARY, 1904

DIED, JACKSONVILLE, ARKANSAS, 1958

and

my friend and colleague

David L. Kubal

1936–1982

If there is no atmosphere, what will it serve a man to demonstrate the excellence of lungs? How much profitabler, when you can, like Abbot Sampson, breathe: and go along your way!

THOMAS CARLYLE, *Past and Present*

The ancients are only venerable to us because distance has destroyed what was trivial; as the sun and stars affect only grandly, because we cannot reach to their smoke and surfaces and say, Is that all?

RALPH WALDO EMERSON,
Introduction to *Past and Present*

What made Wordsworth's poems a medicine for my state of mind, was that they expressed, not mere outward beauty, but states of feeling, and of thought colored by feeling, under the excitement of beauty. They seemed to be the very culture of the feelings, which I was in quest of.

JOHN STUART MILL, *Autobiography*

Contents

Acknowledgments

In the early summer of 1986 I flew to Cambridge on a Travel to Collections Grant from the National Endowment for the Humanities, which made it possible for me to explore an invaluable cache of assorted papers deposited in the Harvard Archives by Bessie Zaban Jones. She generously permitted me total access to the collection. Good friends in Cambridge, William J. and Lia Poorvu, opened their home to me. During that same return to Harvard, after more than thirty years had passed since I studied there, I had the good fortune to confer with Daniel Aaron, Jerome Buckley, and Michael Shinagel—all of whom, in various ways, had been touched importantly by Howard Mumford Jones's personality and teaching. Daniel Aaron kindly lent me his correspondence with Jones. A sabbatical granted by California State University, Los Angeles, my professional home for more than twenty years, enabled me to begin serious work on this project in the fall of 1987.

In the ensuing months, Walter Rideout, James K. Robinson, Arnold Schwab, and Wallace Stegner shared with me letters they had received from Jones. David Levin and Roger B. Stein took the trouble to write personal reminiscences. Jesse L. Cook, Jr., a personal friend of mine and nephew of Bessie Zaban Jones, gave me his impressions. As I moved more seriously into the project, Richard M. Ludwig, who allowed me to make a tape recording of our conversation when I visited him in Princeton, loomed ever more importantly as the man who had known Jones better than, perhaps, anyone outside the family. I was fortunate to have the moral and intellectual support of someone whom Jones himself, in the dedication to his autobiography, had thanked for "affection and support that has run for so many years I know not when it began."

I am grateful to Bessie Zaban Jones and Richard M. Ludwig for their patience, encouragement, wise counsel, and invaluable advice in matters of fact and nuance. Their reading of the early versions of this book prevented errors and oversights and made it possible for me to capture whatever I have of Howard Mumford Jones's mind. Whatever I have overlooked, misinterpreted, or distorted is, of course, entirely my own doing.

My colleague Alfred Bendixen was good enough to invite my participation at a nationwide gathering of Americanists at San Diego in 1989, the Cal State Symposium on American Literature, where I had the chance to test some of my ideas about Jones on a panel devoted to biography and cultural criticism. The chairman of that session, Kermit Vanderbilt, proved to be a generous and insightful confidant, and I thank him for his guidance in the ways of authorship. His writings about Jones's work and the scholarship of other prominent Americanists are invaluable to anyone working in the field.

My understanding of philosophical issues was strengthened in an interdisciplinary graduate seminar I had the good fortune to teach with the philosopher Joseph Prabhu, my colleague. I learned a great deal from him and our students in the English and philosophy master of arts programs.

Once the first draft was finished, in addition to the responses from Mrs. Jones and Professor Ludwig, I benefited greatly from critical readings by Anthony Arthur and Sidney Richman. Ruben Quintero, once my student, now my colleague, and, as reader of this book, a brilliant and humbling "editor," earns a particularly heartfelt thank you.

As a teacher at a university that assigns the heaviest teaching load in upper-division college education in America (but makes up for it by enrolling the most genuine and winning students in the country), I am deeply grateful to the Huntington Library in San Marino. Situated only a few miles from my campus, the library is a sanctuary where throughout the years I have had the opportunity to converse with Allan Casebier, John Steadman, Don Wayne, Paul Zall, and others too numerous to mention; to read in its stately halls and secluded carrels; to meditate on walks in Edenic corners; and to work on this book. I want to personalize my gratitude by thanking Reader Services Librarians Doris Smedes and Virginia Renner.

I also want to thank the former chair of my department, John Cleman, for drawing on the Katherine Carter Faculty Development Fund to defray typing costs and Blanca Arellano and Jean Gee for helping with the actual typing.

My close friend of many years Norman Fruman stokes the mind and heart with ideas and feelings. My wife and children—Nurith, Jonathan, and Moriah—have a glowing presence that makes all of life's difficulties seem secondary. Nurith, a journalist by profession and a teacher of Hebrew, combines that sense of present and past that has helped me keep the greatness of Howard Mumford Jones in focus. I ask her forgiveness for allowing my work on this book to cut into my share of the gardening.

My closing expression of gratitude and indebtedness must go to the Director of the University of Missouri Press, Beverly Jarrett, who believed in this manuscript from its earliest, shaggy days. Her support and the insightful scrutiny and good sense of my copyeditors, Jane Lago and Gloria Thomas, have made this a better book than it was.

* * *

In addition to the very general acknowledgments listed above, I wish to thank Daniel Aaron and Walter B. Rideout for the use of lines from letters to them by Jones. Through the courtesy of the Harvard University Archives (Harley P. Holden, Curator), I have been permitted to use passages from letters by Jones to James B. Conant, Lewis Garnett, and George Sarton. I am also indebted to the Harvard Archives for permission to use material from letters to Jones by James B. Conant and Justin Kaplan as well as a letter from James B. Munn to James B. Conant. I owe particular thanks to Page Stegner for giving me permission to quote extensively from a letter by Wallace Stegner. And I am grateful to Richard B. Stein for letting me quote from his letter to me of reminiscences of Jones.

The following presses and journals have my thanks for permission to use excerpts of some length from their publications: excerpts from *One Great Society,* copyright © 1959 by Howard M. Jones and renewed 1987 by Bessie Z. Jones and Eleanor Ingersoll, reprinted by permission of Harcourt Brace & Company; excerpts reprinted by permission from *Revolution and Romanticism* by Howard Mumford Jones (Cambridge: Harvard University Press), copyright © 1974 by the President and

Fellows of Harvard College; a biographical sketch of Howard Mumford Jones reprinted by permission from *Harvard Scholars in English, 1890–1990,* edited by Walter Jackson Bate, Michael Shinagel, and James Engell (Cambridge: Harvard Faculty of Arts and Sciences), copyright © 1991 by the President and Fellows of Harvard College; excerpts reprinted by permission from "The Terrible-tempered Mr. Jones" by Eric Solomon in *Harvard Magazine* 80, no. 5 (May–June 1978):88–90, copyright © 1978 *Harvard Magazine*; excerpts reprinted by permission from "The Nature of Literary History" by Howard Mumford Jones in *The Journal of the History of Ideas* (April–June 1967) (reprinted from Howard Mumford Jones, *Violence and Reason,* New York: Atheneum, 1969); excerpts from *The Age of Energy* by Howard Mumford Jones, copyright © 1970, 1971 by Howard Mumford Jones, used by permission of Viking Penguin, a division of Penguin Books USA Inc.; excerpts from *O Strange New World* by Howard Mumford Jones, copyright 1952, 1954, © 1964 by Howard Mumford Jones, renewed © 1980 by The Cambridge Trust Company, used by permission of Viking Penguin, a division of Penguin Books USA Inc.; excerpts used by permission from "Prose and Pictures: James Fenimore Cooper" by Howard Mumford Jones in *Tulane Studies in English* 3 (1952) and excerpts used by permission from "Poe, 'The Raven,' and the Anonymous Young Man" by Howard Mumford Jones, which first appeared in *Western Humanities Review* 9, no. 2 (Spring 1955) (both essays reprinted in Howard Mumford Jones, *History and the Contemporary,* Madison: University of Wisconsin Press, 1964); and, finally, excerpts used by permission from *Howard Mumford Jones: An Autobiography* by Howard Mumford Jones, copyright 1979 (Madison: University of Wisconsin Press).

Howard Mumford Jones

and the Dynamics of Liberal Humanism

Introduction

Howard Mumford Jones is both Emerson's "man thinking" and Wordsworth's "man . . . talking to other men."[1] An Americanist who was originally a comparativist, Jones was very much at home in several literatures. He emphasized, without any apologies for what appeared contradictory, the European connection while at the same time acting as a shaping force in the establishment of American literature as an indispensable component of any respectable English program. In his long career as scholar and lecturer, he demonstrated tirelessly that America was an extension of the Atlantic community. Late in life, he qualified this emphasis by urging Americans to become aware of the fact that America shared two hemispheres, the Northern and the Southern, *and* to study the Asian world.

Nevertheless, his position at the crossroads of European and American culture (in a manner reminiscent of Lionel Trilling, who never left his post at the "crossroad of politics and literature") was an eminence Jones never deserted. He stood there in 1928 when he contributed "The European Background" to Norman Foerster's *The Reinterpretation of American Literature* and in 1948 when he wrote an introductory chapter with the same title for the *Literary History of the United States.* Those opening purple paragraphs, so vividly historical, seem to be an effort to derail the entire project from its formalist tracks.[2]

1. Readers who wish an accurate and cogent summary of his life are urged to turn to the Appendix for a sketch written by his peers and students recently published in *Harvard Scholars in English, 1890–1990,* ed. Walter Jackson Bate, Michael Shinagel, and James Engell, 64–67.

2. Kermit Vanderbilt, in his *American Literature and the Academy: The Roots,*

He was still standing at the same crossroads in 1974 when he published his last major work, *Revolution and Romanticism,* a final statement on the connections between American and European culture in the late eighteenth and early nineteenth centuries.

The range of Jones's learning put him at the same level as the great European comparativists who found refuge in America's universities during his career—scholars like Werner Jaeger, Erich Auerbach, Leo Spitzer, and René Wellek. At the same time, his sophisticated grasp of European thought protected him from the kind of risks in advocacy that colored the work of his brilliant fellow Americanist at Harvard, F. O. Matthiessen. Jones knew too much to confound Christianity, communism, and New Critical organicism.[3] In the same vein, although he respected Perry Miller's erudition, that scholar's Puritan monism clashed with Jones's sense of the varieties of cultural experience that had gone into making the American mind. Jones recognized the true genius of a cosmopolitan intellect when he saw it and championed the appointment of Harry Levin, who ultimately strengthened the departmental structure of comparative literature studies at Harvard.

In the growing debate between postmodernism and an aroused humanism, too often, somewhat ironically in the light of postmodernism's burial of the author and denial of a discrete subjectivity, it is the postmodernists who are the individualized players: Derrida, Foucault, Lacan, Kristeva, Greenblatt, and others. The humanists, on the other hand, constitute an indeterminate vapor laced with elitism and flushed with nostalgia for transcendence, a pale "Storm Cloud" of the past. In the opening chapter of his new book, Brook Thomas takes umbrage at the tendency of contemporary scholars to dismiss great mid-twentieth-century humanists with far too cavalier a turning of the page: "Should we lump the work of Erich Auerbach and Leo Spitzer under [Michael] Warner's label of the 'somewhat dreary and encyclopedic historical work that the philologists used to do'? If I could only be so dreary. Rather than hastily consign such work to the dustbin of history, we might use it to pose challenges to our present projects."[4]

Growth, and Maturity of a Profession, 435–37, 499–505, provides important information on Jones's gadfly behavior as contributing editor to the project.

3. Jonathan Arac, *Critical Genealogies: Historical Situations for Postmodern Literary Studies,* 157–75.

4. *The New Historicism and Other Old-Fashioned Topics,* 8.

* * *

Nothing illustrates more sharply Jones's importance as an American authority on European culture than his essay "The Influence of European Ideas in Nineteenth-Century America." It first appeared in 1935 in *American Literature* and was reprinted in Jones's collection *Ideas in America* in 1944. Arthur Lovejoy had delivered the William James Lectures at Harvard on "The Great Chain of Being" in 1933, and his book with the same title had appeared in 1936, the year Jones joined the Harvard faculty. Jones and Lovejoy both had a hand in introducing the cultural complexity of European idealism to American thought. Lovejoy did this by demonstrating how European Romantic writers internalized tropes of being and thereby found release from rusty moorings in theology and rationalism. Jones did it by noting that despite the moral risks ("sensualism, cynicism, and Satanism") of this kind of internalizing, "the really great American moralists—like Emerson, Alcott, Thoreau, and Whitman—were stimulated by exciting philosophical discussion from or about Europe." Jones went on to center this philosophical stimulation in the dialectic operating between the "mechanistic" and the "organic" views of reality:

> It is time, however, to consider the second pole of influence, which I have called the dynamic conception of nature. In this interpretation, which lies between Newtonianism and Darwinianism, and which prepares the way for evolution, the universe is seen in terms of creative energy rather than of mechanical motion, its perfection being the harmony of the Divine Artist rather than the unity of a perpetual motion machine designed by a Great Engineer. The mechanistic view yields to the organic, scientific observation gives only a partial view unless coupled with poetic insight, intuition is found equally valuable with impersonal deduction; and, far from awakening terror because of its vastness, the universe reveals a new and stimulating majesty perpetually active. I suggest that this larger concept draws to a focus such subsidiary forces of European influence as literary romanticism, transcendentalism, the doctrine of immanence, the vitalistic concept of life, and a certain expansiveness, an affirmative optimism said to characterize the American attitude toward living. I do not, of course, suggest the dynamic principle as the sole source of these ideas.[5]

Typical of Jones's scholarly thoroughness, the above passage is but-

5. Howard Mumford Jones (hereafter HMJ), "The Influence of European Ideas in Nineteenth-Century America," 257, 258, 260–61.

tressed by footnotes, three times as long as the passage itself, that include references to Schelling, Goethe, Schiller, von Humboldt, Coleridge, and Carlyle—not to mention the scholarship of Rudolf Haym and Oscar Walzel. The synthesis that Jones achieved here served as a paradigm in American literary scholarship on this question for some thirty years. In 1964 Leo Marx directed readers in search of "the decisive place of the mechanical-organic distinction in romanticism" to M. H. Abrams (1953), Morse Peckham (1951), and the above essay of Howard Mumford Jones, which first appeared in 1935, nearly twenty years before either of the first two Marx mentioned. It is also significant that well into the 1980s Jones's coinage of "the dynamic conception of nature . . . the dynamic principle" held its place in discourse on the intellectual history of this period: "Dialectic thinking . . . sees the world in terms of balanced or alternating and unanalyzable opposites, rather than mathematically measured quantities, and in terms of dynamic process."[6]

Jones's prescience and shrewdness, his willingness to synthesize boldly and then step back urbanely ("I do not, of course, suggest the dynamic principle as the sole source of these ideas"), behoove readers to take a fresh look at his work. There is so much, for example, in what is defined today as New Historicism that he anticipated decades ago. What Jerome McGann, Herbert Lindenberger, Stephen Greenblatt, and others have been telling us about the new referentiality (the need to break down the barriers between literary texts and historical and social phenomena) and the fallacy of historical presumption (that one cannot judge another age while wearing the green glasses of one's own)—these ideas, characteristic of the new discourse in literary history and criticism, were not only adumbrated but often firmly asserted by Howard Mumford Jones.

The following peroration to an address Jones delivered at Cornell University in July 1966 provides the perfect introduction to his theories of cultural and literary historiography:

> Above all—and this is my final plea—literary history is a problem of culture. Writers partake of the cultural, intellectual, and political movements of their time. They know kings and statesmen, painters and

6. Leo Marx, *The Machine in the Garden: Technology and the Pastoral Ideal in America*, 377; twenty years later: Peter L. Thorslev, Jr., *Romantic Contraries: Freedom versus Destiny*, 73.

philosophers, musicians and poets, even generals, clergymen, businessmen, scientists, social workers, and day laborers. They express an age. But an age expresses itself not in poetry only or the drama, the essay, the novel, and literary criticism. It expresses itself in philosophy, the fine arts, international diplomacy, the movements of armies, city existence and country life. Is there no important analogue between the fugues of Bach and qualities of the closed couplet of Dryden and Pope? Is there no living connection between Matthew Arnold's experience as school inspector and his *Culture and Anarchy*? If Emerson's earlier prose is a statement of what later commentators called the "Newness," are not the radical philosophies current in the age of Jackson, the destruction of the United States Bank, the panics of 1837 and 1857 as relevant to Emerson as the truth that he read Swedenborg and Sampson Reed? Is there no conceivable meaning in the fact that Gilbert and Sullivan, Augustus de Morgan's *Budget of Paradoxes,* publication of the collected works of George Riemann, the non-Euclidean geometer, the earlier paintings of Seurat, and those amusing spoofs, *Flatland* and T. A. Guthrie's *Vice Versa,* come along together, all exercises in ingenuity, all denying that any statement of the truth is absolute, all asserting in their several ways that our knowledge of things is relative to the viewpoint of the observer? . . .

To me it is naive for the specialist in the literature of, say, the English eighteenth century to confess not merely that he knows little about the French "philosophes" and the progress of poetry on the Continent, but also that he has little notion of music from Bach through Mozart to Beethoven, no interest in painting from Sir Peter Lely to William Blake, small concern for dress and costume and manners during the century, only a tepid enthusiasm for the literature of exploration, and small ability to cope with the theory and practice of science in that great age. His business, he claims, is with literature and with literature only. Called upon to deliver a manuscript about English poetry from Dryden to Wordsworth, he delivers one impeccable in scholarship, yet blind to eighteenth-century life. Is it to be inferred that members of Johnson's Club were interested only in books? Were they not concerned about the activities of Sir Joshua Reynolds, the astronomical discoveries of Sir William Herschel, papers read before the Royal Society, Lord Monboddo's astonishing theories about language, orangoutangs and the human race, Blackstone's doctrines of law and government, and the eternal puzzle of the female sex? The most superficial reading of Boswell's Johnson denies the queer assumption that authors live only for publishers and for each other.

I hold, then, that literary history, difficult to write and requiring, if it is to be excellent, the kind of patience that brought Gibbon's *Decline and Fall* into being, should be written as the highest form of cultural history; that though individual volumes in literary history now publishing are often excellent works, we still lack a philosophy of the subject; that

> literary history requires the spacious thinking about civilization and literature more common among historians than literary specialists; and that, though our graduate training must still insist upon the elements of scholarship, mature scholarship must in this particular look beyond the monographic concept of research now dominant, towards larger horizons and a richer philosophy about the place of arts in human society.[7]

* * *

Having introduced Howard Mumford Jones's contributions to literary thought in America, I now want to caution readers not to expect a biography. I do begin by sketching some dramatic moments in Jones's life in order to vivify his historical importance, but like Carlyle's Abbot Samson, my Howard Mumford Jones is primarily an example of someone in the "past" who can help us deal with the problems of the "present." I raise the ghost of a strong scholar of the recent past to challenge the present discourse in cultural and literary criticism. While I try to engage various contemporary schools of criticism, there is no attempt to supplant theory with theory. There *is* a hope that in a strong personality whose mind, temperament, and social responsibility were all of a piece readers may see a model for forging a more constructive dialogue between present and past *and* between both of them and the future.

My interest is in Jones's written works, scholarly and polemical. Nevertheless, I have leaned heavily on his autobiography, which he wrote in 1979, one year before his death at age eighty-eight. Despite his age and the discomfort of a muscular disease, Jones tackled the subject of his life with all the saltiness, honesty, and vitality of his best years. He enjoyed the editorial assistance of his devoted student and adviser Richard M. Ludwig. The autobiography does not, of course, preclude a biography. When Jones was awarded the Alumni Medal by the University of Chicago in 1974, the citation, after listing his accomplishments in scholarship and humane education, closed with the following observation: "To write a biography of Howard Mumford Jones would be, in more ways than one, to record the impact of university humanist thought on this country in the last fifty years." Any biography project with hopes of accuracy and scope will require an Ameri-

7. The Cornell address was entitled "The Nature of Literary History" and appears under the same title in Jones's collection of essays *Violence and Reason,* 180–81.

canist trained in archival research and ready to pore through papers scattered from Chapel Hill to Ann Arbor, from the University of Texas to Montana, from Chicago to Cambridge, from the University of Pennsylvania to Wisconsin—not to mention the New York files of the American Council of Learned Societies (ACLS) and, of course, the archives and libraries of Harvard, where my study took root.

For readers who may feel that the inclusion of biographical chapters in a cultural critique centered in a scholar's writings is somewhat out of fashion, I call to my defense the recently published memoir by Alice Kaplan, *French Lessons.* In the long wake of the de Man affair, she, a former student of his, reminds us that when teachers write books and profess ideas, their lives *are* part of the picture.

1

The Call to Harvard

In February 1936 Harvard University President James B. Conant requested the university's Department of English to consider Howard Mumford Jones for an appointment as full professor. Conant also invited Jones to participate in the great pageant of Harvard's tercentenary celebrations, scheduled for September of the same year, where he was to receive an honorary doctorate. This struck many in and outside the university as an odd move. When the list of honorees was announced early in July, Louis M. Lyons of the *Boston Globe* found it "surprising to Cambridge that the one man of letters in America to receive tercentenary honors should be Howard Mumford Jones!" What about "William Lyon Phelps? Thornton Wilder? Sinclair Lewis? Carl Van Doren? Joseph Wood Krutch?" Why should Harvard hand "all her bouquets to a forty-four-year-old English teacher from Ann Arbor?"

James B. Munn, chairman of the English department, was entrusted with assembling an appointments committee. Conant wanted to hire Jones as a "distinguished man of letters." The committee did not seriously question Jones's merits as a man of letters but raised some questions over the possible lack of a fixed focus in his scholarship. To be a comparativist was one thing, but to range from translations of Heine to an importunate essay on *Hamlet,* followed by a study of the connections between American and French culture, and to rush down yet another path with a projected biography of a Romantic poet of the second rank like Thomas Moore—all this perplexed scholars who thought of themselves as guardians of Harvard's conservative tradition of sober and specialized research in literary history and philology.[1]

There was another matter. At the Modern Language Association's annual meeting during the Christmas vacation Jones had delivered a controversial speech, which was to be published in *American Literature* in May. Eight years had passed since the appearance of Norman Foerster's call to arms, his collection of essays by prominent Americanists, *The Reinterpretation of American Literature,* the volume to which Jones had contributed "The European Background." Another contributor to that volume was sitting in Munn's office that day in February when Conant made his request. Kenneth B. Murdock, author of "The Puritan Tradition," knew that Jones's speech at the MLA constituted a declaration of independence, at the very least a "white paper," in a controversy that had been at a rolling boil for a good decade.

Jones began his address by drawing battle lines: "Scholars in the American field are struggling with a well-nigh insoluble problem—a problem created by the attitude of professors of English literature and expressed in the policies of English departments and organized scholarship in this century." The main problem, Jones felt, was that specialists in English literature were encouraged to concentrate on specific periods: Restoration, Romantic, Victorian, and so on. These periods rarely exceeded a century in length and were usually much shorter, and specialists in fiction or drama could confine themselves to a single genre within these periods. Not the Americanist. Expected to deal with "everything from 1607 to 1935," the professor of American literature was responsible for the literary texts, culture, and history of over three hundred years. Small wonder, snapped Jones, that "large portions of the subject receive superficial treatment," causing "the professor of British literature . . . to murmur something about the lack of depth and richness in American literary scholarship."

Despite his passionate insistence on the importance of American students of literature knowing their own literature thoroughly, no one could accuse Jones of indifference to the European tradition. Eight

1. James B. Munn to James B. Conant, February 5, 1936, Conant Papers, Harvard University Archives, Cambridge.

years earlier he had insisted on the centrality of the "European background" to American literature and had even gone so far as to "hesitatingly advance the hypothesis that the difference between Americanism and Europeanism, if there is any, is mainly a difference of rhythm and tempo." In the MLA address Jones was careful to remind his audience that commitment to American literature in no way excluded the study of English writers: "I do not wish to cut off American students from British literature, and if any department were to embark upon so insane a program, I should at once protest. The superior richness of British literature is undeniable."

These were flowers twined around brickbats. Jones's pugnacity, however, could take an acerbic turn. There is a touch of demagoguery in Jones's maintaining that Walter Hines Page had been so thoroughly indoctrinated with the ascendancy of British literature and culture as a student at Randolph Macon College that when Wilson appointed him ambassador to Great Britain at the time of World War I, the man was more sympathetic to Britain's cause than protective of America's interests. One cannot fault English professors throughout the country for being outraged over Jones's suggestion that the snubbing of American literature arose from a lack of patriotism.[2]

The appointments committee deliberated. It decided to forgive Jones the intemperate tone of his speech. President Conant was delighted. Jones had struck the innovative educator as a breath of fresh air. Here was a midwesterner who would balance the New Englanders in the department. Conant also appreciated in Jones the very things that rendered him suspect to traditionalists in literary scholarship: his published poetry and his reputation as a director of student theatricals in Texas and at the universities of Chicago and Michigan suggested there was a private man to balance the public one. Jones's involvement in academic politics in a variety of universities in all major regions of the country might ventilate the offices of the Department of English at Warren House—and perhaps provide a foundation for administrative leadership at Harvard. The chemist in Conant appreciated Jones's intellectual scope and his friendliness to science.[3] Above

2. HMJ, "American Scholarship and American Literature," 117–19, 121; also "The European Background," in Norman Foerster, ed., *The Reinterpretation of American Literature: Some Contributions toward the Understanding of Its Historical Development*, 66.

3. In 1963 Jones coedited with I. Bernard Cohen, the prominent historian of science, an anthology of nineteenth-century scientific prose.

all, Conant valued Jones's reputation as an effective teacher and lecturer; as a reviewer, critic, essayist, and public speaker; as a man who could persuade his students and the community at large of the centrality of the humanities.

Sixty years earlier, Conant's precursor Charles W. Eliot had revolutionized "the physical and academic character of the college." In addition to broadening the curriculum and instituting a wide range of electives, Eliot had brought graduate education to Harvard and attracted an outstanding group of teachers. One of them was Charles Eliot Norton, whose mission was to teach the undergraduates the cultural and intellectual importance of the fine arts. In the 1870s this policy had a rarefied purpose: the civilizing of the genteel class. By 1936 the larger democratic purpose of relating cultural heritage to the social and political realities of a complex society threatened by economic uncertainty and international war required, as Conant's vision had it, a sensibility capable of understanding the American nation as it really was. Jones was Conant's Norton, an earthier version of a cultural hope. After World War II, Conant no longer minced words and said explicitly that teaching, in its most universal sense, was the highest responsibility of the humanist: "The humanist today, as he was five centuries ago, is not only a discoverer but an interpreter, and above all a teacher, whether his pupils be children, young men and women, or adults."[4]

Although it was primarily Jones's cosmopolitanism that attracted Conant, he was also impressed with the MLA polemic when Jones sent him a copy after it had appeared in print. Conant knew that American literature was ably represented in the English department by scholars of the stature of Matthiessen, Miller, and Murdock, but there was something about Jones's energetic devotion to the American experience that struck a new chord. Indeed, Conant was so taken by his newly appointed professor's argument for emphasizing the study of America's past (Jones had quoted Van Wyck Brooks's famous phrase of the need for a "usable past") that he sat down and pulled together some ideas that resulted in the establishment of a special interdisciplinary program in American civilization headed by a committee on which Jones and Murdock would represent literature:

4. Kermit Vanderbilt, *Charles Eliot Norton: Apostle of Culture in a Democracy*, 122; Conant's stress on "teaching" appears in *Education in a Divided World: The Function of the Public Schools in Our Unique Society*, 78.

> I have just read with great interest the article which you sent me last spring about the place of American literature in the curriculum. . . . I think it is excellent and I agree entirely with your point of view. . . . I believe that a scholarly and intensive study of the history of America in the last one hundred and fifty years . . . together with a study of the evolution of modern science and industrialism would provide the unifying point of view in education which everyone is so desperately seeking.[5]

Conant's flattering vindication in August of Jones's stand at the MLA meeting the past winter climaxed a year filled with other heady moments. In the spring, without any advance warning, Jones had been handed two large envelopes by a department secretary as he and several colleagues gathered casually in the outer room of the English offices of the University of Michigan. Jones had been teaching there for six years. The first envelope he opened contained Conant's invitation to become a tenured professor at Harvard at $10,000 a year, a handsome salary in 1936. The second envelope confirmed an invitation to participate in the tercentenary activities, a request to give a speech on the theme of "Authority and the Individual," and the announcement that he, Howard Mumford Jones, was to receive an appropriate honorary degree. Too dazed to note that all these papers were marked "Confidential," he had passed them on to O. J. Campbell, a loyal patron of Jones's and, as it happened, a Harvard Ph.D. Campbell had promptly fallen to his knees "like a Buddhist monk and held up his hands in an attitude of prayer and meditation."[6] Campbell's ironic gesture had bubbled with the good humor of the moment, but it had also underscored with annunciatory power what was happening to Howard Mumford Jones.

When Conant's letter praising his stand at the MLA arrived late that summer, Jones could add to his accolades of the spring firm evidence that his championing of American literature and culture would receive the active support of the most powerful administrator in the world of American higher education. Jones was teaching in the summer session at the University of Colorado in Boulder when Co-

5. James B. Conant to HMJ, August 17, 1936, Conant Papers.

6. HMJ, *Howard Mumford Jones: An Autobiography,* 177. Jones never forgot the delicious comedy of this scene. He would reenact it himself years later in the 1950s when he dropped to his knees before Robert Frost in gentle mockery of the poet's rumored flirtation with the Catholic church. "Viva Papa!" he exclaimed. "Viva Papa!"

nant's letter reached him. He answered immediately and responded to Conant's proposed interdisciplinary program with an affirming battle cry: "It seems to me that the first university which will work out a program of this sort will do more to salvage the college of arts from anarchic disintegration than all the vague talk about culture which is now made to take the place of realistic thinking." Jones wanted Conant to know that he was not aligned with any of the ideologies waging critical war in the 1930s, not the New Humanism of Irving Babbitt, not Southern Agrarianism, not leftist ideologies—not any point of view that threatened scholarly objectivity. His scholarly conscience fed an intellectual commitment to extreme caution in all matters of definitive resolution. *Revolution and Romanticism,* Jones's last major scholarly work, published in his eighty-second year, was described by Robert Alter in a prominent review as suffering from an inability to distinguish "foreground" from "background." What Alter failed to grasp was that Jones's long life of scholarship had not persuaded him that scholars knew enough to divide one from the other, that they had earned the right to impose the principle of perspective on a landscape still very much in shadow.[7]

At the tercentenary activities, one month after he had answered Conant's letter of praise, Jones addressed the same problem in intellectual history that lay at the heart of *Revolution and Romanticism,* written almost forty years later. He thought nothing of wrestling with facts for a lifetime if the generalizations deduced needed refining. "Authority and the Individual," his tercentenary assignment, had been split into four topics, the last being "Classicism and Romanticism," to which Jones contributed a discussion on Romanticism in American literary history. In that address of 1936 he fell back on what he later admitted was "perhaps a rash generalization," namely, that Americans never knew Romanticism in its historical European sense—a phenomenon rooted in the Middle Ages and, throughout the nineteenth century, identified with political reaction. Jones was still evaluating, refining, and correcting that generalization in his eighties.[8]

On the third day of the three-day climax of the tercentenary festivities, September 18, 1936, Howard Mumford Jones received his honor-

7. HMJ to James B. Conant, August 22, 1936, Conant Papers; Robert Alter's review appeared in the *New York Times,* September 8, 1974.

8. HMJ, *Autobiography,* 180.

ary degree. He was eleventh on the list, between Sir Arthur Stanley Eddington, the renowned astronomer and physicist, and Sir John Henry Clapham, the celebrated economic historian; both men were Cambridge dons. Jones's degree was that of Doctor of Letters, the first of fourteen honorary degrees he would receive. The citation read as follows: "An American writer and scholar whose critical study of our own literature assists the country to appraise justly its own culture."[9] Jones was pleased by the simple wording and precision of expression. He could identify with an idea of criticism that bound it to an objective evaluation of the nation's literary past, a theory of criticism subservient to the purpose of cultural self-appraisal. That was his idea of criticism as "realistic thinking."

There is something Johnsonian in Jones's rigorous "self-demand," a scholarly responsibility to "repose on the stability of truth" while in endless awe of fact and nuance. Johnsonian is also Jones's ferocious integrity, projected by a temperament both irascible and kind. And just as Johnson, to this day, has been seen by many to be more moralist than man of letters, Jones had difficulty assuming the mantle of literary scholar unless he could wear it as a responsible historian of phenomena, ideas, and values. He would have questioned the way today's New Historicists dismiss older ideas of the organic integrity of literary texts, but he would have probably agreed with their belief that literary texts are minefields with the same ideological conflicts that pervade the culture itself.[10]

The bulk of Jones's career was dominated by literary formalism, which reached the apogee of its influence in the 1950s when W. K. Wimsatt and Cleanth Brooks published their *Literary Criticism: A History* and Wimsatt laid down the injunction that the literary text must be "hypostatized" as a reified concept. This, however, did not entail any serious attention to the text's historical roots or cultural obligations. Nevertheless, ever since the 1930s some of the most significant literary scholarship of our time has resisted the temptations of formalist theory and asserted the importance of exploring literature's capacity to convey the past's often complex sense of its own presence. Douglas Bush, another of Jones's Harvard colleagues, perhaps even

9. Ibid., 183.

10. My comparison of Jones to Samuel Johnson is inspired by yet another colleague of Jones's at Warren House—Walter Jackson Bate and his *Samuel Johnson,* 296–367.

more learned than he, was skeptical of "historical" reflections by critics grounded in formalist sensibility: "Mr. [T. S.] Eliot has damned most nineteenth-century poets for failing to fuse emotion with intelligence—a theory which may be right, though it can scarcely be proved by quotations from the metaphysical poets at their best and from Browning and Tennyson at their worst."[11]

11. Douglas Bush, *Mythology and the Romantic Tradition in English Poetry*, 533–34.

2

Origins and Aims

Along Came Jones

Howard Mumford Jones rode out of the West in 1936 as something of an ironic Lochinvar:

> I leave here on the 29th August and shall speed to Cambridge as rapidly as I can. Riding over the continental divide on a horse has given me a look (what with peeling) somewhere between that of an Indian and that of a patient suffering from a rare tropical disease.[1]

On horse or on foot he always made an impressive entrance. In his youth in La Crosse, Wisconsin, he strode across Hamlin Garland's front lawn with a self-confidence Garland never forgot. The sandy-haired youth who had been hired to type the novelist's manuscripts eventually became the scholar and personality whose "effectiveness" confirmed Garland's earliest expectations.[2] Striding across Harvard Yard some thirty years after he had first reported to Garland, Jones was now a prematurely balding man who, with his straightforward and brusque manner, reminded everyone that although very much

1. HMJ to Conant, August 22, 1936, Conant Papers, Harvard University Archives, Cambridge.
2. Hamlin Garland, *Diaries*, 161–62.

at Harvard, he was not of Harvard. The midwestern stranger who could match the eastern savants at their own game, Jones felt sincerely humbled at the honor of having been called to Harvard, a position to which he had never aspired; he also felt energized by his difference and persuaded that he must remain true to it. There were some who found his blustering ways and paraded learning overbearing: "Howard Mumford Duck," they called him. Somewhat similar to Mark Twain's problems with New England's illustrious authors (one remembers the disastrous immortal dinner hosted by William Dean Howells), Jones's difficulties with Cambridge decorum served in the main to validate his uniqueness and to stoke his own sense of mission. Conant was farsighted in forcing him on Harvard and Harvard on him.

Behind the triumph of the professorship at Harvard stretched years of struggle. Jones's childhood was basically wholesome but laced with loneliness. His father, who was a genial "drummer," insurance agent, and for a time owner of a pool hall, was bookish, liked stylish clothes, and "would have been happier as a teacher." He died in 1906, when his son entered high school. Mrs. Jones was left with a large house and no income. She became an itinerant hairdresser and massaged the scalps of La Crosse matrons in their own parlors. The boy took on a demanding paper route that kept him busy every weekday afternoon and exposed him to the "tidy" red-light district and its saloons, where he could warm up on cold days and eat at the "free-lunch counter." On Saturdays he "collected ten cents from each customer."[3]

He began his higher education at La Crosse Normal School, went on to the University of Wisconsin in Madison (where he encountered a series of academic personalities: Oscar James Campbell, the first Harvard man in Jones's life; William Ellery Leonard, the poet; and Norman Foerster, Irving Babbitt's disciple), and continued his studies at the University of Chicago. Here more fine teachers came his way, and he wrote for his master's thesis an essay on and translation of Heinrich Heine's great cycle of poems, *The North Sea.* This work was snapped up by the Open Court Publishing Company of Chicago and published in 1916, a year before his degree was officially granted, and reissued as late as 1973. The German customers on his paper route in

3. This and the biographical information that follows in this chapter are taken from Jones's *Autobiography,* 22–23, 48–49, 97, 119, 127–29.

La Crosse a decade earlier, along with the music lessons his mother had provided at great sacrifice, had tuned his ear to the task.

In the same year that he took his degree, he assumed his first academic post, an assistant professorship at the University of Texas in Austin. During the next decade Jones floundered in a series of professional and personal setbacks. First he was caught up in the "Ferguson War," as the vindictive and irrational governor of Texas, James E. Ferguson, tried to cut off all appropriations to the university. Ferguson was finally impeached, but not before the university suffered an interruption in regular funding. Jones's nine-month-old job was in jeopardy when suddenly an unexpected invitation from the University of Montana at Missoula offered an assistant professorship in English at $2,200, more than a 20 percent increase over the salary Jones was about to lose. In less than a year Jones was forced to leave one unfamiliar region for another. The volatility of his professional situation seemed to reflect the turmoil of the day, as America was moving closer to the Great War.

In Montana, Jones enjoyed the grandeur of the mountains, but he soon discovered that an amalgam of mine owners, railroad tycoons, and oil barons controlled the state with a hand no less tyrannical than Ferguson's in Texas. Montana's early history of violent conflict between sheepherder and farmer provided the model for brutal labor wars between the unions and the mining interests in the years Jones taught at Missoula. The same copper interests that lynched Industrial Workers of the World organizers interfered with academic freedom at the university. Without a Ph.D., Jones felt too insecure to ignore a summons back to Texas in 1919 as an associate professor at an increased salary. After Ferguson's impeachment, the Texas legislature had actually increased the university budget. The move to Montana had done nothing to further Jones's career, but it had introduced him to yet another sinewy region of the country. Experiencing the nation in this way somehow supported the perspectives he was developing as a teacher of world literature. Like Frederick Jackson Turner, Jones became sensitized to the shaping power of the western regions in the making of American culture, but it was typical of Jones to refrain from drafting an all-embracing theory of the "receding frontier." Jones, true to his disinclination to generalize prematurely, simply inferred that "the adaptation of European man to a new environment" was being acted out in a drama of great social and cultural complexity. It would require some fifty years of teaching, reflection, and scholarship for him to fully work out this insight.

Jones lingered at Austin, where, on the whole, he made better friends among faculty in history, romance languages, German philosophy, and economics than he did among colleagues in the English division. His intellectual curiosity was simply too broad to be contained in narrow professional corridors. His dramatic temperament found release in the student drama organization, the Curtain Club, of which he had inherited the faculty directorship from Stark Young. Gradually the pressure on him to get a Ph.D. mounted. He took a leave of absence to return to the University of Chicago. With him was the woman from Montana he had married in Missoula. They had a daughter, Eleanor, but the marriage proved unstable. In 1925 the couple separated. Two years later Jones remarried. His second wife, Bessie Judith Zaban Jones, "My Bessie"—as he called her in imitation of Thomas Moore's fond address—became an invaluable collaborator in his research and scholarship.

Before his marriage to Bessie Zaban, Jones had in 1925 reached, in his own phrase, "the dark night of my soul." The difficulties with his first wife were tormenting. Nevertheless, his sense of obligation to the University of Texas kept him at the Harper Library, where he spent long days reading "histories, biographies, autobiographies, travelers' accounts, . . . literary works, anything and everything that had to do with the New World from 1492 to 1848." Whatever the furies that drove him to read so widely, his prodigious memory and unifying imagination never stopped wrestling with the conflicting impressions resulting from his studies. The interplay between American and European culture had possessed his meditating mind with unusual force during his long railroad journeys across the western plains a few years earlier.

His immediate goal was a doctoral dissertation. He focused on the connections between French and American culture from the middle of the eighteenth century to the middle of the nineteenth. Jones's idea of narrowing a topic rarely matched what others thought to be a sufficiently bracketed project. He always needed a large canvas. The Department of Comparative Literature eventually approved his topic, and he applied to the dean of the graduate school to take his Ph.D. orals.

Now occurred an incident that fired Jones's character and put the finishing glaze to a warm but defiant personality. The dean of the graduate school at Chicago insisted that Jones was short on course credits. What outraged Jones was not only the fact that a Ph.D. should be awarded primarily on the basis of course work but also that the dean was asking him to take courses comparable to those he himself had taught in the university's summer program—not to mention the similar courses he had taught at assistant and associate rank at Texas and Montana. The dean remained inflexible to entreaties by Jones and by others on his behalf. So Jones left Chicago without taking his Ph.D. Nor did he ever matriculate at another graduate school. He had the satisfaction, however, of seeing his "dissertation" published in 1927 in revised form at the University of North Carolina, where he enjoyed a happy interval (1925–1930) in the Department of English before moving on to the University of Michigan. The book was largely a critical success except for a demur by Carl Becker, who reminded Jones that "contacts of Americans with things French is one thing; . . . estimating the influence of French culture is another." Be that as it may, *America and French Culture, 1750–1848* remained the standard work on its subject until Henry Blumenthal published *American and French Culture, 1800–1900* in 1975. Blumenthal tipped his hat to his "scholarly" predecessor and judiciously refrained from implying superannuation of Jones's work by altering the chronological focus of his own study.[4] The book that was intended to get Jones his Ph.D., but didn't, remains an authority on its subject to this day.

At Harvard, Jones did not feel disadvantaged without a Ph.D. Ironically, he developed a formidable reputation as a severe examiner on Ph.D. orals. In 1952 he shot off a letter to Lewis Gannett, of the *New York Herald Tribune,* who had surmised that Harvard made life difficult for those who taught there without advanced degrees:

> The great Kittredge had only a B.A. Kenneth Kempton, who is our leading teacher of composition, has, if my memory is right, only a B.A. (perhaps an M.A.). The redoubtable Harry Levin, our chief current exhibit in critical thunder, has only a B.A. I have only an M.A., but the question of a Ph.D. was never raised when I was asked to come to Harvard. And, in fact, in appointments that have come under my eyes in the last fifteen years, the question of a Ph.D. as a mechanical qualification has never come up. Either the man had it or he had counter-

4. *American and French Culture, 1800–1900: Interchanges in Art, Science, Literature, and Society,* ix.

> balancing virtues. But we don't insist on the doctorate, we haven't for fifteen years in my experience, and I think a little looking into the history of the department—take Barrett Wendell as an example—will find other instances. Thought you might like to know.[5]

His lack of a degree remained a badge of honor all his life, proof of his ability to embody the highest professional standards without compromising his own integrity. In 1974 the University of Chicago made amends to Jones by awarding him its prestigious Alumni Medal. Among the many honorific phrases lavished on his accomplishments, the one Howard Mumford Jones must have relished the most is the following: "He has advocated that the civic duty of the humanist is to insist with passion upon honesty, morality, and beauty."

At the Lectern

Howard Mumford Jones had a precise idea of what it meant to be a teacher. He was no educational theorist and could be caustic when it came to expressing his opinions on American pedagogy. When he and Bessie enrolled Eleanor in a local school at the time he was working on his study of Thomas Moore at the Huntington Library under a Guggenheim Fellowship, Jones found, to his annoyance, "that the Pasadena schools were suffering from an attack of that form of educational measles called progressive, or experimental, education." Instead of simply studying French, his daughter was forced to enroll in a six-week course entitled "Broadening and Finding Course in Languages," which consisted of two-week stints in Latin, French, and Spanish. Failing the course as a whole indicated the student was "not adapted" to foreign languages; passing any third of the course meant the student was adapted to that language. Jones noted dryly there was no German. The foolishness of the unexamined assumptions, the inconclusiveness of the findings because of the illogical bracketing of evidence (no German)—Jones found this kind of thinking exasperating. "We argued in vain that we were going to Europe shortly and that French, at least, would seem desirable. We got nowhere. Theory is implacable. Naturally, most pupils found it easier to flunk."[6]

Jones's lifelong aversion to premature or shoddy generalization con-

5. HMJ to Lewis Gannett, January 6, 1952, Jones Papers, Harvard University Archives, Cambridge.

6. HMJ, *Autobiography*, 158.

vinced him that students of all ages had to be trained to respect the significance of important facts. But Jones was no "gradgrind." On the contrary. Facts collided and constantly produced the stuff of humor and wonder. Like Walter Pater, whose impressionist criticism was in vogue during Jones's youth, particularly in the work of James Huneker, Jones trusted not merely "in facts," but "in the sense of facts." In this respect Jones bears comparison to Vladimir Nabokov, his contemporary at the lectern. Both were impressive lecturers; both addressed similar generations of American college students; both saw as their primary mission the sensitizing of their students to an appreciation of "details." To Nabokov this meant "caressing . . . the divine detail."[7] Descriptive nuance in setting, action, and characterization had to be scrutinized with great care in order truly to understand the dominant themes of the literary works in question. To Jones historical and textual details, often minutiae pertaining to little-known or obscure works, were absolutely essential for responsible cultural criticism. Neither teacher, despite a passion for objectivity, is identified with the formalism of his time; each of them believed that literature, although a path with countless turns and markers, led the reader to heights beyond itself. For Nabokov literature was the "magic" door to "pity" and "beauty," to a heightened consciousness. For Jones literature unlocked the mysteries of cultural identity.

* * *

If finally Nabokov's essentially textualist approach strikes us as closer to the New Critical values of Cleanth Brooks and Robert Penn Warren than does Jones's historicism, that is because Jones was definitely closer to the previous century in sensibility and approach. Nabokov was the alienated émigré, a refugee from the nineteenth century; Jones remained an apologist for what he believed was the unappreciated source of our present energies. He literally extolled the nineteenth century. The dynamism and gigantism of the age—represented in everything from its breakthroughs in biology, astronomy, physics, and education to its rediscovery of the literary epic in the form of the triple-decker novel—struck Jones as sufficient achievements to excuse

7. Vladimir Nabokov, *Lectures on Literature,* xiii.

its bad taste, its whorls and puffery, as well as the political sin of imperialism:

> Painting, opera, symphonic music, piano composition, architecture, literature, oratory—everywhere one finds, it seems to me, the same dynamism and flow, the same aspiration and abundance. Consider the prose of Balzac, Emerson, Dickens, Hugo, and Ruskin, the music of Wagner, Mussorgsky, and Richard Strauss, the cartoons of Gavarni, Daumier, Nast, and Tenniel—everywhere fullness of detail, the same lively curiosity, as if nothing had been written or composed or drawn in the world before.[8]

The phrase *fullness of detail* contrasts appropriately with Nabokov's phrase *divine detail.* The author of *Lolita* could not escape the temptations of a form of aestheticism that provided escape from reality and history—or at best ironic transformation of both into the fantastic. Jones leaned in exactly the opposite direction. He historicized with the same intensity that Nabokov aestheticized. Jones would not lose himself in the language or lure of the text if a dimming of historical or cultural awareness was the price to be paid. This put him at odds not only with aestheticism and formalism but also with contemporary literary historicism. New Historicists of several shades question the ability of any interpreter to remove himself sufficiently from his own time to perceive another with anything like the objectivity that Jones felt could be the reward of the truly industrious scholar.

The "fullness of detail" that Jones admired in the nineteenth-century imagination—its "lively curiosity"—was intrinsic to that century's historicism. The "curiosity" principle was at the heart of Michelet's passionately archaeological or archival devotion to the facts of the past, what he called the "reconstitution intégrale du passé," the same idea that von Ranke, Michelet's contemporary, conveyed in his idea of history as grounded in the study of original sources and dedicated to the pursuit of "what in reality has been" *(was eigentlich gewesen ist).*[9] The principle of the "lively" had its origins in Romantic aesthetics and, ultimately, theories of evolution. Jones combined all of this in a somewhat oxymoronic ("lively curiosity") conception that joined factual objectivity and original subjectivity, "abundance" and "aspira-

8. HMJ, "The Greatness of the Nineteenth Century," in *History and the Contemporary: Essays in Nineteenth-Century Literature,* 41.

9. Christian Gauss, *The Papers of Christian Gauss,* 293.

tion" in a meliorist vision. Those who trusted in the facts of Nature and History without relinquishing "dynamism" and "flow" were agents of liberation. Jones had read his Goethe, George Eliot, and, of course, Emerson, who had taught him that "scripture should be taught in the spirit in which it was intended." Facts could set you free; in any case, to be without them guaranteed enslavement. This is what prompted Jones's insistence on the importance of undergraduates *and* graduate students learning and retaining information many of them thought obscure.

It all started with Miss Heidemann, Jones's high school American history teacher in La Crosse. The following passage from his *Autobiography* reads like an allegory for his own life as a teacher:

> I cannot pass the entire staff in review, but in memory Miss Lena Heidemann, who taught American history, was tops. She was an old maid, tall, thin, and angular. Her nose, that rudder of the mind, was of a commanding style, and her eyes could subdue you with a single glance. She had innate dignity, and she expected dignity in others. She also possessed that mysterious quality developed in certain personalities of subduing you without arousing resentment.
>
> The interval between classes was seven minutes, during which time you were supposed to have proceeded from one room to another. Usually there was a buzz of conversation and some mild horseplay even after the teacher had entered the room. Not so in Miss Heidemann's course. The moment she opened the door, conversation ceased, and we respectfully watched as she marched to her desk, wrote a name or a date on the blackboard, turned and surveyed us, announced the assignment for the next session, repeated it for the benefit of the slow of wit, and then proceeded to the business of the hour. If the topic was, say, the French and Indian wars, and if she called on you for information about the battle on the Plains of Abraham, you were expected to answer with precise information. Either you knew that the British general was named Wolfe or you did not. If you did not, she did not scold; she merely gave you a silent glance, and passed on to someone else. She occasionally expressed verbal approval of a good answer, and that made your day. She had complete command of her subject, she was not afraid of dates, she did not surmise that by requiring you to know something precise about the American past she was smothering "creativity." Writing had to be exact and clear, and how many hours she spent reading our slovenly prose I shudder to contemplate. She violated all the rules or rather lack of rules for schooling nowadays, and we adored her for the simple reason that she assumed as a matter of course that she was there to teach and we were there to learn. She remained a fixture of the school for years; when at last she retired and it was learned that her legal pension would not keep her in comfort, some sensible person in La

> Crosse wrote to as many of her former students as he could locate, explained her situation, and asked for contributions. The response was instant, and the checks were accompanied by letters of appreciation.[10]

In Miss Heidemann's command of her subject, her stressing of facts and accuracy, her indifference to the pedagogy of creativity, and her passion for exact and clear writing, Jones found a lifelong model. This was not a model designed to make him popular with twentieth-century students; nor did it help him to earn the respect of colleagues who prided themselves on their ability to go beyond mere specificity in their scholarship. Students and educators, however, who truly understood him realized that "Howard Mumford Jones was an enemy of narrowness, of the assumption that for scholars, a preoccupation with arcane detail could be a legitimate end in itself. His own preoccupations were large: the organic wholeness of the humanities, the education of a responsible citizenry, the human condition."[11]

Jones felt strongly that the higher goals of the humanities could not be realized without educational rigor. Tolerance and openness to ideas had to be developed in the student's mind by an educational process that worked against the grain of the average young person's solipsism and indolence. It was sentimental of educational theorists to believe that encouraging a student's individualism by diluting the complexity of the curriculum could effectively educate a democratic society. The best way to open the mind to the joy of tolerance was to fill it with a barrage of significant data and stimulate the memory to retain it. What intelligence and wit could eventually do with such ample stores—therein lay the hopes of any intellectual culture that education might help bring into being.

Some readers may find the above ideas offensive, if not jejune. In addition to their old-fashioned notion of adolescent character, they exude strong whiffs of elitism and insensitivity to the social complexity of today's educational challenge. In addition, one might very well be taken aback by the dated ideas of perception and cognition implicit in Jones's thought. He seems excessively identified with associationalist psychology as developed by Locke, Hartley, and, finally, William James. We must remember, however, that empiricism is a rich tradition and that its permutations have been somewhat cyclical. In the last

10. *Autobiography*, 36–37.
11. "Howard Mumford Jones," *Harvard Magazine* (July/August 1980): 88.

twenty years we have abandoned phenomenology for indeterminate hermeneutics, and now we seem to be heading back again to a sense of facts in time—elusive nevertheless. My point is that Jones's stubborn rationalism and historical objectivism cannot be dismissed as intellectually irrelevant in a period in the history of thought when flux and faddism hold the chalk. Jones himself knew too much about the history of modern ideas to be overly impressed by any one generation's intellectual banners. The truth is that he had more trust in modern science than he did in modern philosophy, and this helps to explain why he put his trust in facts. For Jones, in an age of science, facts constitute the bread and butter of the intellectual banquet. The humanities cannot teach that age its manners without sitting at the table; the humanities, in other words, have to transcend the narrow specializations of the sciences while at the same time matching their tough-mindedness. "No teaching-training formula can be substituted for the central truth that any proponent of the humanities (at any level of instruction) must be a person of steadily deepening culture," wrote Jones in 1962, "precisely as any teacher of science must be a person of steadily deepening knowledge of science. I think the American difficulty is that we will not, in the humanities, face this issue."

Miss Heidemann *knew* her American history; her grounding in the subject made her credible. She was able to inculcate in her young pupils a respect for the facts and clear thinking that had validated her own pedagogical authority. In a very basic sense, Jones felt that her sound and extensive knowledge was itself the primary enabling factor; that knowing what to teach obviated knowing how to teach; that the method of teaching was only the genie trapped in the bottle of the subject. Educational theorists and behaviorists may question the logic of this assumption. If the method and the knowledge of the subject are identical, why are so many people who have the facts totally incapable of teaching them? That, Jones would answer, is largely a question of temperament. But the corollary of the above, namely, that people who are not fully grounded in the facts and knowledge of a subject can teach it through the instrument of a pedagogy grounded in the principle of creativity, struck Jones as absurd. He simply did not feel that encouraging students in their creativity was as effective as persuading them of his own credentials for making intellectual demands on them. This resulted in a performatory kind of teaching that often intimidated. Jones was an immensely convivial and generous man, and he could be a caring friend to his students. In the classroom, however, he did not seem to worry about being loved. His were the ministries of beauty and fear: the facts were beautiful, and his power over them commanded awe.

Rejecting the benevolence and permissiveness central to almost all post-Rousseauistic pedagogical theory, Jones held out to the end of his professional career for the no-nonsense authority of the informed schoolmaster. Here he is commenting on the "writing" problem in American education in the mid-1960s, the time of his retirement:

> "Today," said Dr. Jones, "you simply write. This is known as creativity." He quotes a well-known American novelist who said "I write to find out who I am," an answer Dr. Jones thinks would have puzzled Shakespeare.
>
> "Writing," he added, "is no longer a difficult craft, the English language is no longer an exquisite tool of accuracy. Writing has become therapy, a form of self-expression. Its mandate is no longer to communicate but to create."[12]

Postmodernists may smile at Jones's confidence in the "accuracy" of language, which, we are told, is categorically identified with "indeterminacy." Jones would have insisted that you cannot teach anything indeterminate; what you teach has to have the hardness of a "tool," the efficiency of a "craft." He was not indifferent to ambiguity and knew that literature was its great apologist, but the subtleties of literature's meanings were finally predicated on the student's awareness of all the facts attending the possibilities of meaning—facts of allusion, history, intellectual context, language.

Communication of facts struck Jones as particularly important at Harvard. He knew he had some of the best minds in the country in his classes in American and British literature. These were students capable of original thinking, subtlety of insight, and, yes, creativity. More than anything else, he feared that these good minds might hover in an intellectual vacuum. If the "facts" did not resonate in the classroom, then they would indeed rust in the musings of antiquarians.

Eric Solomon remembers the following:

> Boy and man, I studied under Howard Mumford Jones, and not only had he read everything ever written and remembered it all, but he also made the student (or quiz-taker) feel remarkably incompetent for lack

12. "Be Obscure, Clearly."

of reading and remembering. He also taught me more than did anyone else at Harvard.

Now, no one ever argued that the Jones teaching technique was subtle. In his huge undergraduate course in American literature from 1890, he hurled fact after fact at us from the moment we arrived at the Fogg lecture hall and glanced at two absolutely jammed blackboards, crammed with details and dates, until he completed his rich oratorical outburst of literary and historical desiderata. The only moments of silence on the part of the indefatigable lecturer came when an unfortunate student arrived after the anointed starting time of seven minutes past the hour. Professor Jones would stop in midsentence, even in midsyllable, and remain silent until the student, embarrassed and stumbling under what was truly a baleful stare, would somehow disappear into a seat. Then, and only then, would the voice of Howard Mumford Jones ring out and complete the word.[13]

Teacher or pedant? Bully or mentor? Jones provided little opportunity to those who would have preferred a neutral or less polar judgment. He demanded a strong response and he got it. He conscientiously pressured students to meet his own standards for research, study, and retention with a thoroughness that fed on a deeply felt liberalism. He was one of the first teachers of American literature to include, regularly, significant works by black writers such as Paul Laurence Dunbar and Booker T. Washington.

Long before Edward Said accused Western scholars of coloring Asian experience in the tainted ink of "Orientalism," Howard Mumford Jones had attacked English departments for being unduly influenced by nineteenth-century German scholarship, which was heavily identified with racist ideas of Anglo-Saxon superiority. His distrust of "tribalism" in all its forms encouraged Jones's comparativist inclinations and made him urge his students and graduate assistants "to look and read voraciously and not to make premature distinctions of quality before [they] had read it all." What Jones wanted to cultivate in his classes and among his protégés was ingrained disinterestedness. This disappointed some students because he didn't always "push through to explore in depth the dynamics of the issues" his own learning had raised. And yet, his teaching allowed others the opportunity to be their own theorists, to be "creative" *in camera*.[14]

13. "The Terrible-tempered Mr. Jones," 88.

14. Maxwell Geismar, *Rebels and Ancestors: The American Novel, 1890–1915*, 391, men-

In 1940 Jones published and distributed to students in his introduction to British literature survey course a fifty-one-page syllabus entitled *Handbook of Instruction,* which by September 1941 had already gone through four editions. By any professional standards, this syllabus was an astonishing performance. In addition to subjects of study such as The Popular Ballad, Elizabethan Verse, and The English Bible, page citations for every class meeting for two terms, and detailed information on evaluation and grading, the syllabus provided chapters up to ten pages long on such subjects as "The Study of Literary History," "Reading," and "Literary Terms." A contemporary instructor would perhaps be most bemused by Jones's insistence that students take lecture notes in a prescribed manner and in a certain kind of notebook. He distinguished between lecture notes and reading notes, and he required the latter to be recorded on one side of a five-by-seven-inch card in a predetermined format. These cards were often collected by section leaders and graded.

In recitations at department parties or at holiday gatherings for students and friends at his home on Francis Avenue, Jones delighted in dramatic displays of his mnemonic powers. He often found ways of using this gift to both intimidate and inspire (depending on your point of view) his graduate students. Solomon recalls a graduate course on the Pre-Raphaelite poets:

> There were about twenty of us, as I recall, each responsible for a cluster of sonnets from the more than hundred poems making up Rossetti's long sequence *The House of Life.* A student would start to explicate a particular sonnet; Howard Mumford Jones would interrupt, "But why do you keep looking down at your book?" Since this was early in the course, the initial student response would be "Well, I want to refer to the text." Looking like an incredulous brown owl, Howard Mumford Jones would throw back his head, stare at the ceiling, and, in a voice that was a cross between a flow of honey and the shifting of gears of a Mack truck, recite the entire sonnet. For each student. Twenty times. And by then he had us, we were his, and Mr. Memory could make us believe anything about Victorian poetry.[15]

In his undergraduate lecture courses Jones tended to do all of the speaking, but in his graduate seminars he would assign reports, which

---

tions Jones's unhappiness with the German influence; in a September 15, 1989, letter to the author of this study, Roger B. Stein shared his impressions of Jones as a teacher.

15. "The Terrible-tempered Mr. Jones," 90.

mellowed with the years and usually made fewer demands on memory than the class Solomon remembers. These reports required the student to display the same qualities Jones stressed in his own lecture courses: generous detail, relentless accuracy, historical background, and clear and organized explication and delivery. In 1937 Jones was actively guiding the doctoral program in American Civilization that Conant had asked him to help set in motion. Among the first graduates of that program, in 1940, was Henry Nash Smith, who was to become a giant in the field of American Studies.

> As a graduate teacher, Smith insisted upon thorough research and regarded precision as imperative, though without being pedantic about it. After Tony Tanner took a seminar from Smith, he wrote an account of it as a model for British universities. Tanner described how the group of students were initially puzzled by the variety of apparently extra-literary projects they were set, such as locating the popular ideas of science in the period under consideration, the nature of book illustrations, the size and distribution of the reading public, and the psychological assumptions of the periodical critics. But later, as they read the fiction together, Tanner said that they came to realize the rich density of understanding they had already accumulated as a group.[16]

It was Jones who from his earliest years at Harvard had assigned graduate students reports on "extra-literary" topics such as "The Influence of Mahan's Work on Sea Power" or "The History of the Land Grant Colleges." His conviction that the study of literature had to serve cultural understanding to justify its place in the college curriculum, and that literature could not accomplish this if studied in isolation, moved him to establish interdisciplinary approaches within the English and American literature curricula. He was not always patient enough to wait for the historians, philosophers, and scientists involved in the American Civilization Program to take a comparativist initiative in their own courses. Hence he used his literature seminars to establish the interdisciplinary standard he felt was vital to the success of the program.

Indeed, the interdisciplinary spirit struck Jones as vital to the survival of culture in the modern world. Being an American was simply another way of being a culturalist. What was a culturalist? Not what most Americans thought such a person to be; Jones indulged his sar-

16. Richard Bridgman, "The American Studies of Henry Nash Smith." Tony Tanner's account of Smith's teaching could also serve as a description of Jones's methods.

donic side in an address to Harvard alumni gathered in Chicago in 1938: "I represent French irregular verbs and the essays of Matthew Arnold. I embody what all red-blooded Americans regard as the decorative and useless element in a college curriculum. I merely represent culture." But then he pulled himself together and suppressed the harshness of his irony. Remembering that his audience was, after all, composed of Harvard graduates and that they all cared about what he cared about, Jones ended his address with the following plea for an interdisciplinary and cosmopolitan philosophy of higher education:

> The chief hope for the humanities in American universities is their recognition of a common aim. That aim is a concern for the history of the ideas which are of most consequence for the human race, not merely those which flatter national vanity.
>
> If in the universities we continue indefinitely to study literature and philosophy and language and the other humane subjects as disparate topics, each in its separate field, no one having a connection with any other; if we do not agree that the history of thought as a whole is our common province, particularly as this relates to our duties as Americans having a belief in liberal culture in the liberal state, not only will the humanities sink to the level of antiquarianism, but we shall have no check upon the misuse and misunderstanding of the products of research in the humanities. . . . As I see it, the humanities have it as their duty to examine all possible interpretations of history and art in the hope that there will arise from the discussion of differing points of view eventual common values to which, in Jeffersonian language, the wise and good of the earth may rally.

Tribune

Many believe Howard Mumford Jones would have made an excellent university president. He liked power and enjoyed wielding it with perhaps too wide a swath. As dean of Harvard's Graduate School of Arts and Sciences during World War II, he wanted desperately to make "radical alterations" in programs of graduate training in the humanities.[17] Even with Conant's support, Jones discovered that his authority was limited. Chafing under university bureaucracy, he grew increasingly abrasive and made enemies. After approximately a year at the job, he came back to the English department unchastened. Veterans returning from the war soon persuaded him that his ideas for

17. HMJ to George Sarton, August 23, 1943, Jones Papers, Harvard University Archives, Cambridge.

graduate reform were too important to give up just because Harvard was not ready for them.

Jones believed that the same interdisciplinary policies that defined the American Civilization Program had to be established throughout the graduate school. Specialization was, of course, essential to graduate study; nevertheless the cataclysm of the war made it all too clear that national cultures should develop a greater tolerance of and interest in each other or all of civilization would collapse. Graduate schools, Jones felt, must not only ventilate the curriculum but also pay greater attention to preparing the graduate student for the professional realities of teaching and research. With important assistance from his wife, Bessie, Jones put his ideas into a series of three lectures that he delivered to the Rushton Foundation in Birmingham, Alabama, in April 1946 and published in the same year under the title *Education and World Tragedy.*

As president of the American Academy of Arts and Sciences and chairman of the Weil Institute, Jones acquired administrative prestige in the 1940s and 1950s, while Harvard chose not to offer him further administrative opportunities outside the English department and the American Civilization Program. Harvard's loss became a gain for the American Council of Learned Societies (ACLS). From 1955 to 1959, as its chairman, Jones was able to play a role commensurate with his considerable gifts for organization and persuasion—a role worthy of his steadfast dedication to the principle that society needs the humanities to be itself.

In four years Jones revitalized the organizational structure of the ACLS, moved its headquarters from Washington to New York, solicited and got huge endowments from the Ford Foundation and the Carnegie Institute, and gave the council a new agenda. In a letter of condolence to Bessie Jones after her husband's death in 1980, George Winchester Stone described Jones as "the man of endless energy and intelligent activity [who] singlehandedly rescued the ACLS from its dying gasp." Jones convened a special commission of academic and business notables to produce a document that would explain what the ACLS was all about to well-meaning but puzzled captains of industry and their "organization men." After a memorable three-day session in 1956, which crowned a series of monthly meetings held during most of 1955 and 1956, the commission agreed to authorize Jones to write the report, published as *One Great Society* in 1959. The following prefatory passage sums up what Jones felt was the main purpose the commission had in mind when it sent him to his typewriter:

> A philologist cannot hope to compete with an atomic physicist for acclaim or for support, nor does this report make any such assumption. It does assume, however, that there is a limit of neglect below which a great nation cannot afford to sink its support of humane learning. This book is intended to help restore balance, not in the sense of taking his money away from the scientist or his key position in government or business from the social scientist, but in the sense of indicating that, wonderful as science is and influential as are the social sciences, they are not the whole of culture. Thoughtful scientists and social scientists never argue that they are. But that portion of the public which is essentially concerned about the drift of American values is not perhaps as fully informed about the theory and practice of humane learning as it would like to be; and it is to such citizens that this volume is directed.[18]

Strengthening the connection between "values" and "learning" continued as Jones's priority in humanism when he accepted the presidency of the Modern Language Association in 1965, three years after his retirement from Harvard. He did his best to democratize the unwieldy structure of an organization suffering from, as he put it, "the forces of multitudinousness and gigantism." He advocated a revival of the regional MLA meetings, a policy reflecting not only his preference for organizational simplification and efficiency but also a deeply felt sympathy for the uniqueness of America's regional life, a sympathy nurtured by the professional wandering of his formative years. He also urged a reform of the sessions, or literary meetings. As constituted, they did not, he felt, permit ample time for discussion. The excessive number of papers read at any one session usually taxed the patience of the audience. Two papers, carefully chosen, should be commented on by a panel of "four or five . . . each of whom [is] assigned some aspect of the subject . . . to lead but not to monopolize discussion."[19] This is essentially what he had been doing in his own seminars for thirty years.

The loosening up of the MLA's roster of topics—a policy heartily endorsed by Jones—eventually took a political and ideological turn in the 1970s that went beyond Jones's intentions. It was not his insensitivity to politically reactionary ideas that had made him invoke Mat-

18. *One Great Society: Humane Learning in the United States,* ix.
19. HMJ, "The Pygmy and the Giant," 8, 11.

thew Arnold's sense of "culture" in his presidential address at the MLA in 1965. Twenty years earlier he had carefully outlined the unfortunate "working interrelation between the Arnoldian doctrine of culture and the Arnoldian belief in racial snobbery and anti-democratic political action."[20] What worried him was the substitution of an "anthropological" idea of culture for the historical humanism underscored in Arnold's equation of criticism with "disinterestedness." Jones's great effort in the 1950s to reinforce the important differences between the humanities and the physical and social sciences through a revitalized ACLS had sensitized him to the dangers of a society excessively reliant on the scientific mind for its idea of culture. Jones admired science, but he shared Arnold's view that it could not supply culture's need for "beauty and conduct." The readiness of "science" to supply answers, hard and theoretical, to all the questions culture poses often tempts passionate political valorization. The heady connection between ideology, politics, and much of contemporary critical theory seems to support Jones's anxieties on this point. Indeed, contemporary historians of critical thought have fallen back on Arnold, albeit with reluctance, for reasons that Jones would have predicted. Here is Jonathan Arac as apologist for Arnold in 1989: "In recovering Arnold as critic and activist, I have tried to specify his goals and concerns enough to make evident that they are no more than partly ours. To accept the Arnoldian 'definition' of criticism is only to prolong a dead yet dominant force. To accept the Arnoldian 'challenge' for criticism requires both seeking different goals and finding different means."[21]

One suspects that Jones would have pressed Arac for a sharper explanation of the difference between his bracketed terms *definition* and *challenge*. He would have found it dangerous to distinguish too sharply between cultural elitism and cultural democracy. His commitment to interdisciplinary approaches spoke for his respect of the sciences, even as he insisted that they were not the "whole of culture"; and he was just as adamant in his belief that topical and popular culture were legitimate meat for the humanist scholar to chew—so long as he was given the right to assume that not everything was worth swallowing. Like Roy Harvey Pearce, Howard Mumford Jones

20. *History and the Contemporary,* 118; the essay "Arnold, Aristocracy, and America" was originally published in *American Historical Review* 49 (April 1944): 393–409.

21. *Critical Genealogies,* 138.

appreciated the dialogue between elitist and popular culture but rejected the dominance of "mass culture."

The important thing was tolerance. Any voice that presumed to interfere with intellectual freedom was unacceptable. Openness, directness, bluntness: these constituted Jones's religion. In the 1930s and 1940s he practiced it fervently; he wrote an open letter to Adolf Hitler, urged Franklin Roosevelt to tell the American people the truth about the inevitability of war, fought censorship by taking the witness stand on behalf of a bookshop indicted for selling the lascivious best-seller *Forever Amber,* and attacked the trustees of the Boston Symphony for their anti-Semitism.

Perhaps his greatest political moment was in the early 1950s when he took on McCarthyism and the academic loyalty oath. To discharge professors for refusing to answer the questions of committees investigating communism was, said Jones, a "shocking and arbitrary act." In an address at the annual Wellesley College Honors Convocation on March 16, 1953, he insisted that to harass the professoriat in this manner constituted "the true threat to academic freedom" by placing "a premium on the informer" and punishing the person "who does not believe it right to endanger the fortunes of other persons in the profession." Like many who challenged McCarthy, Jones found himself subject to vicious condemnation by self-acclaimed patriots. A legislator in West Roxbury demanded his resignation from Harvard: To call patriots "informers" was a stab in the back to our boys in Korea and a "disgusting exhibition of professional irresponsibility."

As the McCarthy probes intensified, Jones interpreted the nation's capitulation to the senator's methods as proof that Americans had become distrustful of the Enlightenment thought supporting their own democratic traditions. "When this country was founded . . . almost everyone believed in a rational universe. What seems to have happened is that we have abandoned this notion of rationality."[22] Almost twenty years later Jones invoked the same principles in condemnation of radical student demonstrations. In April 1970, when students had seized Lawrence Hall, he told one of his former students, the distinguished Americanist Daniel Aaron, "Don't come to Harvard. . . . It is sorrowful to me to see Harvard degenerating, but degeneration is patent."

22. Jones, address to Hadassah Convention, Washington, D.C., October 1953.

All his life Howard Mumford Jones was a spokesman for the university, for what Jacques Barzun has called "The House of Intellect." He believed strongly in the need of the university to meet the social and vocational challenges of the day, but he believed with equal ardor in the importance of standing by culture, of preserving the liberal traditions of the modern university as established by Humboldt in Berlin and embodied in Jefferson's hopes for the University of Virginia. The university was a bastion of hope and tolerance, perhaps the only institution in the modern world where "subjectivity" need not take on the collectivized consciousness that Jurgen Habermas has identified as the modern condition; where, to revive a distinction made by Carl Becker, a liberal historian of Jones's own generation, "ideas" can be distinguished from "ideology." When Jones's friends felt he had become something of a reactionary in his old age because of his extreme position on student rebellion, they failed to see the consistency of his liberalism. Anyone who undermined the modern university was undermining the best hope of the modern world. Long before the student turbulence had crested in the late 1960s, Jones irritated graduate students at Harvard by questioning their moral claims on the university for financial support of their studies. When they complained about the needs of their budding families, he shot back that they had no right to expect the university to encourage their self-indulgence. Certainly, this has an outrageous ring, but it also reveals his love of dramatic statement and ironic exaggeration. The truth is that he personally helped students. The subtext here is something like this: Finish your studies before you marry and breed. Scholarship is a jealous mistress. You have greater obligations to the House of Intellect than it has to you.

The "G.I. Bill Ph.D.'s," many of whom were Jones's students and were, in many cases, the academic power elite at the time of the Vietnam and civil rights protests, vacillated between dedication to the institution that reified their own hopes after World War II and sympathy for the political iconoclasm of their students. Unlike Jones, who belonged to a generation reared in progressivism, tempered by the Great Depression and the war against fascism, they did not, finally, have a fierce trust in education as social and cultural deliverance.

3

The Grand Alliance: Criticism and History

His dedication to the university as a bulwark for humanism in the modern world drove Jones to what may strike contemporary educators as a bias against creativity. The reader will remember Jones's skeptical distrust of the pedagogical value of stressing creativity in the classroom. Our democratic culture, he felt, was better served by the cultivation of a widespread cultural intelligence than it was by the false promise of universal genius. We have seen how Nabokov and Jones used literary detail for different purposes. Nabokov wanted to intensify his students' appreciation for the nuances of literary creativity; Jones wanted to intensify their grasp of cultural complexity. In a complimentary review of Alfred Kazin's *On Native Grounds,* Jones wrote, "[Kazin] has . . . no theory . . . except that literature ought to mean something to mankind. Too many writers talk as if men exist for books."[1]

It is true that Jones was persuaded that historicism provided the student firmer ground than what creativity promised. However, he felt this way for reasons that went far beyond questions of pedagogical strategy. Art, he came to understand,

1. Review of *On Native Grounds,* 5–6.

immolated itself to culture in order for culture to understand itself. Art, because of its very nature, cannot know itself. It is a great Dionysian mystery and constantly eludes binding definition as to origin, substance, and effect. Jones taught himself this truth about art in lifelong ruminations on Romantic aesthetics and post-Enlightenment thought. For him, culture was defined by art, even if art could not define itself. Not always delighted by their difficult union, culture and art were nevertheless inseparable. The zeal of certain contemporary theorists to establish parity between the powers of the creative artist and the creative powers of the literary critic would have struck Jones as profoundly wrongheaded. What led the literary critic to interpretive discourse was precisely his deficiency in creativity, his innate separation from the nescience that thinkers from Plato to Poe have correctly identified with art. The critic's sensitivity to historical values allows him to pursue a cognitive course of inquiry largely denied to the artist. If, however, literary art proves ultimately resistant to critical analysis, the critical effort is redeemed by what literary criticism teaches us about culture.

In his influential essay "The Historical Interpretation of Literature," Edmund Wilson argues for the historical influences of art in a discussion heavily indebted to Hippolyte Taine and then leaps, in his conclusion, to the position that finally the evaluation of art turns on ideas of order.[2] In other words, one can describe a work of art only in cultural terms, but to evaluate it, one must have an aesthetic system. Jones does not make this leap because he is persuaded that all we can finally evaluate is the degree to which a work of art serves a cultural purpose.

This does not mean that we cannot look closely at the text. Indeed, Jones could roll up his sleeves and deal with the particulars of a text with as much industry as Cleanth Brooks or Jacques Derrida. In 1955, Jones felt compelled to rebut W. H. Auden's attack on "the general faultiness of Poe's verse." The great example of this faultiness, it seems, is "The Raven." Jones did not agree with Auden's conclusion that "the thematic interest and the prosodic interest, both of which are considerable, do not combine and are even often at odds." Jones does agree with Auden that the poem lacks the "natural flow" of language suit-

2. In *The Triple Thinkers: Twelve Essays on Literary Subjects,* 257–70. The essay was originally delivered as a lecture at Princeton University on October 23, 1940.

able to the speaker and the situation. The redundancy of alternatives ("stopped or stayed he"; "lord or lady") is fed by a crushingly frequent use of feminine rhymes "rare in English," according to Auden. Jones, however, feels that the grotesqueness of the prosody is essentially a reflection of the speaker's state of mind. That mind is not of the lover-persona Poe himself posits in "The Philosophy of Composition" but is in fact that of a more generalized and symbolic figure representative of the cultural *Zerrissenheit,* or dislocation of the age. Here it is best to have Jones speak for himself:

> Obviously it is a poem about an Anonymous Young Man. Now the Anonymous Young Man is a standard nineteenth-century hero. He suffers a great deal, especially in the first half of that immortal epoch, so much, indeed, that I cannot recall any literary work in which he is truly happy. He paces the shores of the sounding sea in "Locksley Hall," uttering a variety of morbid sentiments, and he goes mad in "Maud." His odd goings-on are chronicled by Bulwer-Lytton, Dickens, and Disraeli. He turns up in Matthew Arnold, he turns up in Clough's "Dipsychus," and he turns up as the thoughtful young man contemplating the harlot in Rossetti's "Jenny," as William C. De Vane has sympathetically demonstrated. He goes abroad, too, and writes the confession of a child of a century with the pen of de Musset, and becomes a stoic with de Vigny. As an Italian he laments the brevity of life with Leopardi, as an American he is sensitive in Hawthorne, as a German he haunts that literature from Tieck through Heinrich Heine. Sometimes he has a name, but essentially he is anonymous. Elderly critics might refer to him as a stereotype, but contemporary refinement likes to call him a *persona*—a mask through which the writer speaks as a poet, not as a man.
>
> Whether stereotype or *persona,* the Anonymous Young Man is a signal to the reader. He is not an ordinary, middle-class young man, well adjusted to society, comfortable in his religious beliefs, persuaded of the bourgeois virtues, and modeling himself upon Benjamin Franklin. The Anonymous Young Man is sensitive, morbid, and accursed. He likes to prowl around at night. He likes to experiment with drugs, hypnotism, music. Sometimes, as in the case of Bulwer's Pelham, he manages to throw off his doom by embracing a radical philosophy (in this case utilitarianism), but more commonly, like the modern Private Prewitt, his abnormality is so fixed, he embraces darkness like a bride. Unlike that unfortunate bugler, the Anonymous Young Man is much given to study, seeking in strange libraries some answer to the riddle of the painful earth. And always (again unlike Prewitt) he is confessional, not, I think, because of any "destructive passion of the lonely ego," but mostly because he just likes to talk. When, therefore, a reader in the

> 1840's picked up a new poem called "The Raven," he knew at once it was about the Anonymous Young Man:
>
> Once upon a midnight dreary, while I pondered weak and weary,
> Over many a quaint and curious volume of forgotten lore—
>
> And as the detective story fan immediately asks himself, "What's the new gimmick in this one?" so the reader, when American taste was thus low in 1845, asked himself, "What is novel, what is strange about the Anonymous Young Man this time?" He read "The Raven" with certain expectations in mind. He expected the poet to establish a new variant in the psychology of the Anonymous Young Man.

How, asks Jones, does Poe succeed in turning the "Anonymous Young Man" into a "monomaniac living in a surrealist universe"?

> The process is that of hypnotizing both the Anonymous Young Man and the reader, and to this hypnosis the meter, together with the iteration of a few significant symbols inextricably caught up into the meter and coming relentlessly around with it, is the chief contributor. Obviously one such symbol is "tapping," which, with its synonym, appears eight times. Another such is "Lenore," which also appears eight times. A third, a little more difficult to define, is the element of light in the poem, in its struggle with darkness and light. . . . The meter holds together superbly the two elements that compel a willing suspension of disbelief until the poem is done—namely, the grotesque and the maniacal; and I do not see, once one has mastered the true theme of the piece, that the prosodic interest and the thematic interest are anywhere antithetic, but rather that they are one and indissoluble. I am sure Poe sincerely believed that in "The Raven" he was celebrating that most melancholy of themes, the death of a beautiful woman, but the saintly Lenore is never described, and all that we know about her is that she is with the angels. What is presented, and powerfully presented, is, however, the movement from sanity to monomania in the "soul" of the Anonymous Young Man of the period; and this is managed by prosodic devices so powerful that nobody has since dared to imitate them.[3]

This long passage conveys much of what is at the heart of Jones's method. Although he seems to be paying lip service to the conventional critical wisdom of his day—New Critical organicism—it is clear that what really interests him is the way in which the cultural typology of the "Anonymous Young Man" dominates the poem despite

3. *History and the Contemporary,* 153–55, 158, 160. The essay is entitled "Poe, 'The Raven,' and the Anonymous Young Man." It first appeared in *Western Humanities Review* 9 (Spring 1955): 127–38.

Poe's own explanation of his speaker's intentions. Contemporary readers may note the way Jones flirts with what we now call reader-response theory; others will see in his handling of the question of meter an anticipation of deconstruction—and certainly many will want to call his "Anonymous Young Man" a semiological phenomenon. No matter what critical sensibility we bring to our reading of his commentary, Jones always leaves us pondering questions of historical and cultural significance, what Everett Carter has underscored in Jones's own phrase, "history of sensibility."[4]

He was always adept at criticism and had a feel for its *jouissance* that would have pleased Roland Barthes. Instead of encouraging feelings of autonomy and liberation from history, however, *jouissance* made him skeptical of the intellectual and cultural significance of criticism itself. Much of this difference between Jones and today's literary thinkers is of course attributable to the fact that Jones's generation, in its youth, found hope in modern history, whereas Barthes saw little in it but betrayal and hypocrisy. Yet Jones never had illusions about history. He was not reassured by soft-minded ideas of progress; nor was he overwhelmed by the social Darwinism of his formative years, although he always had a weakness for powerful reformers like Theodore Roosevelt. So did Walter Lippmann, who maintained that Theodore Roosevelt was the only president for whom he ever felt a personal fondness. With Lippmann, as with Jones, to be liberal was to have ideals and hope, and for both men modern history provided evidence that their ideals and hope had some foundation in the facts of man's experience.[5]

Early in his career Jones indulged in a form of *jouissance* that taught him, once and for all, the limitations of criticism. At Texas and later at the University of Michigan he was active in theatrical productions. In 1918, at the age of twenty-six, he published a monograph at the University of Texas (where he held his first academic position) entitled *The King in "Hamlet."* He approached *Hamlet*, the play, as a problem in dramaturgy. He could not accept the dramatic exaggeration of the character Hamlet, an interpretation based on received critical wisdom in place ever since Coleridge, which diminished other characters in the play, particularly the usurper King Claudius. To grasp fully the play's

4. Everett Carter, *The American Idea*, 3.

5. HMJ, *The Age of Energy: Varieties of American Experience, 1865–1915*, 393–95; Ronald Steel, *Walter Lippmann and the American Century*, 63–64.

dramatic conflict required a richer understanding of Claudius than the traditional fascination with Hamlet's character permitted. To be actable the play had to be more than Hamlet's. To make his case, Jones argued that the play is more than a family tragedy: it is a royal tragedy. Claudius is a murderer, but he is a capable monarch, apparently more gifted as a ruler than Hamlet's bellicose father. Through a detailed analysis of the text, Jones suggested that Claudius is an underestimated character, that the king's "ethical problems" are important: "Now in all that I have said, if I seemed to depreciate the importance of Hamlet, it is not my intent, but because Hamlet has overwhelmed the play. Hamlet is the hero of his tragedy. But to make Hamlet interesting does not require that we make Claudius unreal. Far from helping Hamlet, we have damaged the tragedy in so doing."[6]

Written some seventy-five years ago (and four years before T. S. Eliot's "Hamlet and His Problems"), this ingenious piece of criticism anticipated by twenty years not only the organicist assumptions of New Criticism but also more recent discussions representative of New Historicism.[7] Although strenuously analytical, the essay is also consciously tendentious and almost comically self-aware in the way Jones seems to straddle his own argument. In short, the *jouissance* of the project is the source of its energy. Jones perceived what he was doing as a sport: criticism comes out the way the critic wants. And Jones wanted to underscore the play's theatricality with its inherent, structural dramatic conflict regardless of the effect on our grasp of the thematic complexity conveyed in the words and thoughts of Hamlet himself. Aware of the critical liberties he had taken, Jones tried to strengthen the case for a rehabilitation of Claudius by stressing his transformation of Denmark into a hereditary monarchy, which would have been seen as "politically correct" by Queen Elizabeth. Through history Jones hoped to improve what he knew was not a disinterested critique. His real intention, his ideology, in other words, was dramaturgy. He argued that history provides a kind of insurance against what ideology may cost. And in this case, the moral cost is high. Claudius, regardless of his political suitability, is a scheming murderer.

History, for Jones, had more to offer than the supportive assurance of strategically useful facts. History includes intellectual history, and

6. *The King in "Hamlet,"* 97.
7. Leonard Tennenhouse, *Power on Display: The Politics of Shakespeare's Genres.*

Jones had very strong ideas on how it should be done. As I have noted previously, Jones could not separate literary and cultural history, and indeed intellectual history combined them both with a philosophical power. As Emerson wrote, and Jones repeatedly quoted, "Scripture should be understood in the spirit in which it is conceived." We cannot ignore the past's sense of itself. Jones came to recognize that "to linguists now it seems the utmost absurdity to try to fix a language for all time; nevertheless the Academy, by its very existence, declared that style is the morality of art. Style is a civic responsibility, not an individual idiosyncracy." In the greatest historians that "civic responsibility" avoids "idiosyncracy" through a form of sympathetic identification that Jones might have compared to Keats's "negative capability": the quality that enables poets to lose themselves in their creations. There is a lurking contradiction in the way Jones, who usually distinguished sharply between "communication" and "creativity," attributed poetic powers to the historian who reaches philosophical insight:

> The writers are steeped in information, they live backward, they are themselves imaginatively involved, they are participants in the disastrous expedition to Syracuse, or sit in his studio with Velasquez, or struggle with the dark powers of stupidity and sin with Jonathan Edwards at Northampton and Stockbridge. They do not write out of sentimentality, they do not, as the phrase goes, "appreciate" the art of literature or the beauties of science, they do not turn Jefferson's first inaugural into a moral lesson in tolerance and American idealism. They are superior to this naiveté. They are so steeped in knowledge, they have passed beyond particulars into philosophy, they live, as it were, double lives—one in the present tense, and one, intelligent, informed, vital, philosophic, human and sometimes humorous, in that portion of the human story that has claimed and riveted their attention so long, they cannot exist without expressing in orderly prose its greatness and its importance.[8]

Howard Mumford Jones lived his erudition. It transcended the text before him in the sense that he could not ignore what his historically educated memory brought to the fore when his mind was presented with a problem in literary interpretation. Jones conflated historical and critical response: "Whenever literary criticism neglects history, it grows absolute and inhuman."[9]

8. *Revolution and Romanticism,* 19; also his *Violence and Reason: A Book of Essays,* 177–78.

9. *The Theory of American Literature,* 118.

It would be incorrect to suggest that contemporary deconstructionist criticism "neglects" history. Indeed, Jones's emphasis on the relationship between history and criticism is reversed when deconstructionists argue that too strong an embrace between them has produced exactly the results Jones feared their separation could bring about. Deconstructionists urge us to confront in the language of literature the traps historical language has itself created. Barbara Johnson, a prominent deconstructionist, in her brilliant essay "The Execution of Billy Budd," closely examines the text of Melville's last great fiction as an exploration of cognitive and ethical ambiguity: "It is a dramatization of the twisted relations between knowing and doing, speaking and killing, reading and judging, which make political understanding and action so problematic." The following illustrates her perception of Melville's ambiguity:

> Melville's choice of the word *marplot* to characterize the originator of Billy's stutter deserves special note. It seems logical to understand that the stutter "mars" the plot in that it triggers the reversal of roles between Billy and Claggart. Yet in another sense this reversal does not mar the plot, it constitutes it. Here, as in the story of Eden, what the envious marplot mars is not the plot, but the state of plotlessness that exists "in the beginning." What both the Book of Genesis and *Billy Budd* narrate is thus not the story of a fall, but a fall into story.
>
> In this connection, it is relevant to recall that Claggart falsely accuses Billy of instigating a *plot*, of stirring up mutiny against the naval authorities. What Claggart is in a sense doing by positing this fictitious plot is trying desperately to scare up a plot for the story. And it is Billy's very act of denial of his involvement in any plot that finally brings him *into* the plot. Billy's involuntary blow is an act of mutiny not only against the authority of his naval superiors but also against the authority of his own conscious intentions. Perhaps it is not by chance that the word *plot* can mean both "intrigue" and "story." If all plots somehow tell the story of their own marring, then perhaps it could be said that all plots are plots against authority, that authority creates the scene of its own destruction, that all stories necessarily recount by their very existence the subversion of the father, of the gods, of consciousness, of order, of expectations, or of meaning.[10]

Johnson uses biblical mythology to provide a suprahistorical dimension for her meditation on the meaning of "plots," a meditation rooted in semiology and driven by a clever milking of lexical ambi-

10. *The Critical Difference: Essays in the Contemporary Rhetoric of Reading*, 108, 87–88.

guity. The effect is to totalize the elusiveness of cognition. We cannot connect stories with meaning because plots themselves are defined by myth rather than literary history and words are never just what they purport to mean.

For Jones *plot* cannot be displaced from its historical origins. It is a word brought into literary discourse by Aristotle, not an emanation hovering over Genesis. Indeed, Aristotle's idea of *plot* (*mython*), despite the suggestion of its Greek etymology, resonates with the important distinction it establishes in Western thought between history and poetry. History can never enjoy poetry's ability to focus on a single action freed of random qualities and realized in mimetic plausibility. Johnson's deconstruction of "plot" ("intrigue" and "story") turns it into a subverted history of itself and suggests that its irrational shadow—what modernity calls myth—has engulfed Aristotle's original intention to distinguish not between rationality and irrationality but between the plausible (*mimesis*) and the implausible (*historia*). For Aristotle, the historian Herodotus was not a poet, or maker of plots, because he did not make "an imitation which is unified and complete in itself and which is governed by narrative or dramatic causality." Jones's historical frame of reference made clear to him that plot, as Aristotle understood it, was not used for fiction until well into the eighteenth century; that its traditional literary home was primarily the drama and, only in a marginal sense, biblical narrative. This fact struck Jones as powerful evidence of the transforming pressures of sentimentalism on late eighteenth-century comedy. It was remarkable that cultural forces could detach the drama from its roots in Aristotle's "causal" idea of plot, that neoclassicism could dissolve at its center. When commenting on Diderot's comedies, Jones emphasized the irrelevance of plot to the meaning of the plays. "I repeat, the plot is of no importance; the point is that all parties in this touching scene [the "conversion" scene in act 5 of *Le Père de famille*] act from the highest sentimental motives."[11]

For some readers the advantage of Johnson's method may be that it seems to take her closer to the text, and the disadvantage of Jones's that he seems to desert the text to illustrate shifts in sensibility and culture. But a second glance might alert the reader to the fact that Johnson's analysis is less faithful to the text itself as an entity than it is

11. Timothy Steele, *Modern Poetry and the Revolt against Meter,* 118; HMJ, *Revolution and Romanticism,* 106–7.

to the word *marplot,* that her narratological perception—"a fall into story"—is anchored in the importance of one word to the entire story.[12] Jones, on the other hand, takes the trouble to translate the scene in question from French into English, a lexical analysis very different from Johnson's semantic focus, and tries to provide its essential flavor, its mise-en-scène.

But are not the words of the text its primary source of meaning, whatever "meaning" may be? Yes, if we have that meaning in historical focus; no, if we do not. "Meaning is not simply a matter of response but is determined by historical factors which can be known and presented as evidence," argues Wesley Morris, who goes on to remark, "Howard Mumford Jones notes that one of the most immediate problems facing the literary historian is 'whether literary history is to be encyclopedic or selective.'" Jones never forgot that the historian could not presume to the "causal" structures of the poet. Jones's critics would argue that he never solved this problem, but then neither has anyone else. Only recently has deconstruction reversed itself on "history" and become passionately encyclopedic in its pursuit of historical, *not* linguistic, minutiae to save the literary reputation of Paul de Man, a reputation central to the survival of the school. In another development, New Historicists of all persuasions seem to have discovered a selective kind of literary-historical criticism that begs the question of any real difference between a broad or a narrowed focus on actual texts. Minutiae of incident, custom, and design have been turned like skeleton keys to open entire rooms of literary and/or historical meaning, but often the reader is left with the uneasy feeling that evidence is insufficiently objective; that what has the air of encyclopedic neutrality is often unconsciously selective; that polemics and close reading, always problematic allies, have become eerily indistinguishable.[13]

In a late chapter of *Revolution and Romanticism* entitled "The Roman-

12. In another essay, "The Frame of Reference: Poe, Lacan, Derrida," Johnson questions the validity of the kind of overfocused referentiality that she herself seems to be practicing in the essay on *Billy Budd:* "To cut out part of a text's frame of reference as though it did not exist and to reduce a complex textual functioning to a single meaning are serious blots indeed in the annals of literary criticism" *(The Critical Difference,* 116).

13. Wesley Morris, *Toward a New Historicism,* 22; David Lehman, *Deconstruction and the Fall of Paul de Man,* provides the background to the de Man controversy, and Don E. Wayne a useful description of "The New Historicism" as it took shape in the late 1980s in his essay of the same name, which he allowed me to see before it was published.

tic Rebel" Jones brings to a head a discussion in which he has been meditating on Romantic attitudes toward action and will, what Johnson calls "the twisted relations between knowing and doing." Jones cites Marcel Brion's *Allemagne Romantique* (1962) in connection with commentary on Heinrich von Kleist's *Prinz Friedrich von Homburg* (1810):

> [Brion] seems to regard Kleist as virtually a somnambulist, and finds in his plays a dialogue between two states of being—what is possible and what is desirable. Art is a kind of somnambulism, in which the unconsciousness evokes and eventually discharges (as action) what the consciousness is directed to do. The only explanation for the queer state of being in which Prinz Friedrich finds himself when that play opens is a kind of self-hypnosis, which is later to dictate to him his rash action at the battle of Fehrbellin, June 18, 1675. The drama begins on the evening before the battle. The prince is a cavalry leader. The Electoral Prince of Brandenburg-Prussia has made a most careful and thoroughly Prussian plan of battle, which, indeed, brings victory over the Swedes. Instructions to the several divisions of his army are particular and minute, and it is specified that Prinz Friedrich and his cavalry are not to move from their posts without exact orders to do so. But when the play begins, the prince is discovered seated in a sort of trance under an oak tree in the palace garden weaving a laurel crown of victory. He can scarcely be aroused; and when he attends the general staff meeting he hears, but does not take in, the orders of battle. At what seems to him a crucial moment in the struggle, he suddenly gives the order to charge, an attack which routs the Swedes and in fact ensures victory. But he has disobeyed orders; the Electoral Prince declares that he must be court-martialed, and the sentence is death. Pleas to spare the prince are made to the Elector by various personages, including Natalie, who loves him, but the Elector will not yield unless Friedrich himself concedes the justice of the military sentence. The conflict is therefore between the discipline of earth and the sudden insight of genius, a conflict within the soul of Friedrich himself. Friedrich tears up the petition for clemency signed by many, which the Electoral Prince has given him to read, and announces his decision: "I shall suffer the death sentence which has been passed upon me. . . . Be still! It is my determined will. I will honor the sacred law of war, which I violated, through a death freely elected on my part in the sight of soldiers" [Jones's prose translation].
>
> At the last moment he is pardoned. Before American readers dismiss this *coup de théâtre* as a thoroughly Prussian ending, let them remember that the dilemma of *Prinz Friedrich von Homburg* is like the dilemma of *Billy Budd,* the difference being that Melville sternly sends Billy Budd to execution whereas Kleist spares his erring prince. The philosophic point is that the transcendental rebel can be subdued, pardoned, or punished only by his own transcendental will.

In Johnson's commentary Billy Budd, like Claggart and Captain Vere, is simply swallowed up in the indeterminism that haunts the gaps between performance and "cognition," which in turn seems to condemn "judgment . . . to ground itself in a suspension between textuality and referentiality." Jones, on the other hand, substitutes "will" for "cognition" and thereby not only injects a historical sophistication that liberates the ambiguities of *Billy Budd* from an exclusively textual referentiality, but also establishes a resolution of the "plot" through which Billy Budd's heroic character remains uncompromised. Defined through the typology of a certain kind of Romantic Rebel, Billy, as protagonist, dominates over his two antagonists, who become the instruments of his "transcendental will." Both the Prinz and Billy will their deaths in public ritual in defiance of all forms of judgment, including the ambiguities of the texts in which they live. Many will, of course, question such a reading even when they are reminded of the centrality of the Romantic Rebel with "transcendental will" to Melville's other works.[14]

"Cognition" does not stress character with the same force as "will." The truth is that "cognition" subsumes character to action by implying that action is the result of knowledge. From Sophocles to Beckett, drama makes clear that action may be the result of ignorance—or, put another way, the *illusion* of cognition seems so central to dramatic plotting that to probe its metaphysical ambiguity, in modern narrative *or* traditional drama, is merely to labor what is generically obvious. Recent theories of literary structure have been so caught up in the paradigmatic flexibility of plot that they have underestimated the historical significance of Romanticism's challenge to the dominance of plot over character. *Billy Budd* does not, finally, "fall into story," as Johnson suggests; if it falls anywhere, it falls into character, not plot; into "will" powerful enough to "transcend" cognition rather than bow to its imperatives. Jones had a rich sense of the irrationalism at the heart of great nineteenth-century texts, and as much as he disliked that irrationalism, he never failed to perceive its consequences.

Howard Mumford Jones not only trusted in the past as a source for the information and ideas that would enable him to interpret great literary art, but he also believed that holding on to the legacy of humanism was the best insurance against cultural and social decline.

14. HMJ, *Revolution and Romanticism*, 389–90; Johnson, *The Critical Difference*, 104–9.

We have seen how these ideas influenced his teaching and politics. It is as an Americanist that Jones's humanism underwent its greatest test. To put it as simply as possible, he knew that a "usable past," in Van Wyck Brooks's phrase, was an absolute necessity if civilization was to prosper in America. As a trained comparativist and student of European culture, he also knew that America could not afford to relinquish its ties to the European past. What he set out to do was demonstrate how American culture was equipped to carry out the best hopes of European culture, but in an idiom entirely its own. America could not afford to confuse its uniqueness with separation from Europe. What it had to discover and explore was its capacity to carry the European heritage to heights denied the Europeans themselves. "The United States was conceived by intellectuals who thought in terms of the Enlightenment; and though men like Adams and Jefferson were more pessimistic about human frailty than legend allows, they believed this republic could live only on a principle of rationality."

As modernism took root and Jones, in his long life of involvement in American culture and education, watched it come into threatening bloom, he grew increasingly anxious that America's unique cultural mission to bring European humanism to its greatest perfection might fail. Jones was too close to the heartland of America to share with any great anxiety the fears of people like H. L. Mencken and Sinclair Lewis, who in the 1920s insisted that America's greatest threat came from its own provinciality. Jones was confident that education would eventually contain the "booboisie." What he feared was that American sensibility would succumb to European modernism (which he understood historically as the stepchild of a decadent Romanticism) and thus betray its historical mission: the realization of the Enlightenment dream of a rational and moral society. Ironically, then, he felt that America was closer to the spirit of Western humanism than cultivated and decadent Europe. America was with the ancients, Europe with the moderns. When Jones delivered his presidential address at the Modern Language Association's annual meeting in 1965, he echoed Jonathan Swift's attack on the spider, Swift's symbol of the moderns, for the "good plentiful store of dirt and poison in [its] breast":

> Today, especially since Santayana's *The Genteel Tradition at Bay,* idealism is a pejorative term, and rationalism is replaced by ego-projection, alienation, the creative unconscious, and anguished self-analysis, but

> until after World War I the data of greatness—that is, masterpieces of art and thought supposed to possess timeless validity, were the substance of literary study, and language, the noblest instrument of man, was analyzed as rational discourse.

Three years before his election to the presidency of the MLA, Jones had retired from Harvard. Although seventy years old, he had yet to publish the first of his three major works. This happened in 1964, the year before he made the MLA presidential address. *O Strange New World: American Culture, the Formative Years* was a critical success and earned him a Pulitzer Prize. He stood there at the lectern in December 1965 the self-conscious representative of a whole range of ideas he knew most of his audience considered entirely out of date: "I hold . . . that the principal duty of the Association is to do all it can to enrich culture through scholarship, and I unashamedly use culture, not in the anthropological but in the Arnoldian sense of the word." What gave him the confidence to take this culturally conservative position was not only the success of his recently published book but also the knowledge that, barring ill health, his learning would see him through to a successful confrontation with modernism. He was skeptical of its accuracy but gave some credence to the notion that "mathematicians and scientists are said to burn out earlier than do humanists and historians." And he took strength from the works of his favorite neglected American poet, who in the last decades of his long life produced such memorable lines as these:

> The night hath not yet come; we are not quite
> Cut off from labor by the failing light;
> Something remains for us to do or dare;
> Even the oldest tree some fruit may bear.

If the contemporary reader cannot abide Longfellow, let him contemplate Hegel, who asserted that the owl of Minerva takes wing at twilight. Finally, even more than his own self-assurance, the growing conviction that modernism had exhausted itself gave Jones the greatest hope.

He had strong support for this belief in the work of Lionel Trilling, whose criticism he had reviewed favorably in the 1940s and 1950s. In the MLA address Jones noted that in his recently published collection of essays, *Beyond Culture,* Trilling recorded his students' blithe acceptance of modern literature's "subjective morality" at face value and no longer seemed able to associate reading with social and cultural criticism. "Teachers . . . may one day have to question whether in our culture the study of literature is any longer a suitable means for developing and refining the intelligence," predicted Trilling.[15] Jones pounced on this as evidence that the nation was betraying its Jeffersonian heritage and rose to the following admonition: "If Trilling is right that literary studies can no longer be thought a suitable means for developing and refining the intelligence, then the theory of the Modern Language Association is wrong and must fail." Jones could not have known how the younger radicals squirming in their seats in 1965 would in 1970 interpret this admonition in political terms far to the left of what he had in mind. He was right about the malaise of modernism, its diminishing fascination with its own "anguished self-analysis," but he underestimated its hatred of the past. Trilling had, perhaps, a greater insight into the heart of the dilemma, namely, that modern subjectivity depended on alienation for its identity and could not turn to culture or history for solace without betraying itself. This was the sober idea Trilling struggled with in *Sincerity and Authenticity* (1970), which he delivered in its original form as the Norton Lectures at Harvard. Jones sat in the audience.

Gradually Jones became more tolerant of the unavoidable blend of rationality and irrationality in the modern mind. The closing chapters of *Revolution and Romanticism* (1974) bring him to a dialectic similar to Trilling's, but such thinking represented an accommodation that went against the grain of his strongest convictions, which he reasserted in the last pages of his *Autobiography,* written a year before he died:

> The uncritical acceptance of a shallow doctrine of human nature as fundamentally irrational . . . is now the stock in trade of the arts, and, unfortunately, of many humanists, and is flatly contradicted by the dazzling success of rationality in other fields. Poets and novelists, filled with zeal for irrationalism, inconsistently continue to go to the dentist, the doctor, and the surgeon for physiological repair on scientific principles discovered by rational research.[16]

The year 1965 was memorable for other reasons. Earlier in the year he had written a postscript to his influential *Theory of American Literature,* originally published in 1948. While the original volume had at-

15. Lionel Trilling, *Beyond Culture: Essays on Literature and Learning,* 232.
16. *Autobiography,* 273.

tacked tendentious historians like V. F. Calverton, a Marxist, and Ludwig Lewisohn, a Freudian, it had shown respect for Vernon L. Parrington and his great predecessor Moses Coit Tyler, who had written about American literature as the record of a people coming into cultural and social identity. Jones had cited the historiographical principles of A. W. Schlegel and Mme. de Stael: literature revealed the soul of a nation. The making of culture was *the* literary enterprise. These thinkers were strongly identified with German Romanticism, and Jones had risked contradiction in applying their ideas of how literature can express the spirit of an age or people to his own sense of America emerging in an essentially Enlightenment and thus rationalist mode. Perhaps his conviction that rationality lay at the heart of Western culture had enabled him to gloss over the fact that his historiography was relying on Romantic theories hostile to its essential rationalism.

By 1965 the contradiction was apparent. Jones could no longer tout his Jeffersonian model for American literary sensibility in the face of the overwhelming evidence that American writers—from Jonathan Edwards to William Faulkner—had, as he noted himself in his MLA speech, an irrepressible "zeal for irrationalism." The truth is that he had always known this to be true. The ideologue in Jones resisted what the scholar had come to know, but the scholar eventually prevailed. In important ways, the scholar had already raised his voice in 1948. Although Jones had been emphatic in his endorsement of what he called the "central fact in Bacon's essay ["De Augmentis Scientiarum"] . . . that literature is a social act," he posed a series of questions for the literary historians of the future that invite a close look at the subjective and darker side of the unconscious mind:

> Are there continuing concepts of beauty and grace expressed in American writing that historians of ideas do not recognize, because they are myth and symbol rather than notion and argument? Why, if the smiling aspects of life are the more American—and Howells was a shrewd observer—is our literature so curiously marked by melancholy? Why, in a gregarious people, this loneliness of the soul? and, among a kindly one, these sudden imaginative rushes of violence, brutality, horror, and despair, mirrored in imaginative writing?

In the postscript of 1965 Jones began to answer some of his own questions, but he did so defensively. The scholar faced the evidence, but the ideologue permitted himself an acid tone of renunciation: "The concept that a representative republic should per se create a unique republican culture has virtually vanished from the twentieth century." In other words, although American literature had achieved sufficient sophistication to embrace modernism, it was in danger of losing its birthright: "A country that produces *Tropic of Cancer* and *Candy* as a kind of equivalent of the fiction of Céline would seem to have given up pretending to a special moral or aesthetic or intellectual virtue of its own."[17]

Why was Jones so bitter over the country's flight from the vision of its founding fathers? After all, as he himself had noted already in 1948, it was "increasingly evident that the United States has become the heir of Europe in that transit of civilization our political historians delight to trace." With the rise of America to world prominence, seemingly the most powerful society and culture on the planet, Jones could have fallen back on his arguments of twenty years past. At that time, in his contribution to Norman Foerster's *Reinterpretation of American Literature* (1928), in an essay entitled "The European Background," Jones had written, "American letters cannot be wholly 'explained' either by reference to themselves or by reference to American history. Something is lacking. That something is a constant reference to the cultural fact that America is part of the west-European world."[18] Now that postwar America had reasserted that European connection by taking the lead in championing modernism, why could Jones not make his peace with the course of history? The answer to this last question is complex. It has a great deal to do with the social and political forces at work in American experience between the two wars, forces that Jones feared were simultaneously promoting elitism in the arts and condemning the American public to vulgarization by the mass media.

Jones ended the 1948 edition with a meditation on the importance of critics and historians finding a common ground:

> The historian must of course concern himself with the elements of nationalism in the national letters, but he must learn from the critic how to maintain detachment, sympathetic yet just, from the very element that might otherwise enslave him to the state. He cannot, in the present posture of affairs, agree that any state will do; nor does it follow, in the present posture of affairs, that only the American state and only American literature will do. He will, however, if he be wise, learn from the critic (provided the critic be wise) that the distinction between first-

17. *Theory of American Literature*, 13, 182–83, 205–6.
18. Ibid., 171; Foerster, *The Reinterpretation of American Literature*, 64.

> class work and inferior work can never be blurred, if history is to be useful; but he will not, because much American writing is not first-class, therefore infer that the history of American writing is useless to "culture." For if the critic and the historical scholar cannot forget their recent quarrel long enough to tell us how adequate (or inadequate) democratic culture has been in the fostering of literary art, and if they cannot unite on the central problem of evaluating the literary art with which American writers have made their appeal to American men and women, we are in danger either of falling helpless into the mass "media" notion of culture, useful to the police state, or else we shall march farther along the road to Byzantium than most educated Americans care to go.[19]

The importance of not permitting critical values to cloud historical assessment; the need to convey the impact of literature on a generation in its time even when that literature is no longer considered vital by the generation writing the history; the necessity of remembering that literature never exists in a social vacuum (Jones was unprepared to grant the modern artist the stateless condition of a Kafka protagonist)—all these ideas were at the heart of Jones's debate in the 1940s with Robert E. Spiller, one of five editors of the *Literary History of the United States,* first published in 1948. The exchange between Jones and Spiller and much important background information on the compiling, writing, and editing of the *LHUS* have been recorded by Kermit Vanderbilt.[20] Spiller was pleased to have secured Jones's assistance as an advisory editor; he enjoyed his testy letters, but it was clear that the two men disagreed over basic perceptions of what should or should not be stressed in an all-encompassing literary history.

Spiller's theory of cycles divided American literature into two plateaus of literary accomplishment: the years 1830 to 1870 and "the resurging expression of modern times" in the 1920s. Jones felt that this

19. *Theory of American Literature,* 186–87.

20. *American Literature and the Academy.* In addition to detailing Jones's involvement in the *LHUS* project, Vanderbilt provides an excellent "profile" of Jones (448–51), which readers will find a useful supplement to the essay from *Harvard Scholars in English, 1890–1990* that appears in the Appendix to this volume. Vanderbilt correctly stresses Jones's historical importance as a reviewer of "American literature in the making—from Hemingway, Faulkner, and Dos Passos to Lewis, Sandburg, and Cather. . . . Before and into his years at Harvard, Jones wrote constantly his penetrating and fearfully candid reviews of the American criticism or scholarship of Babbitt, Brooks, Eliot, Foerster, Lewisohn, Kazin, Murdock, and LHUS coeditors Canby and Williams. In Canby's *Saturday Review* alone, Jones contributed more than one hundred reviews by 1943."

kind of historical categorizing legitimized what was essentially a critical assessment rooted in New Critical formalism and organicism, a critical approach that had made an impressive marriage with historicism in F. O. Matthiessen's *American Renaissance* (1941). Jones had no great quarrel with New Criticism, and, on the whole, he admired his colleague Matthiessen's accomplishment. But Jones did not think it was the job of literary history to rewrite the past with the critical preference of the day; the literary historian had the obligation to educate his own critical bias with the past's sense of itself.

As Vanderbilt tells us, Jones stubbornly refused to bend to the "cycle theory" even after Spiller had graciously submitted to revisions. Jones kept insisting on an approach that would do greater justice to the valleys; there was too much lingering on the peaks for his taste. He was particularly disturbed by the underestimating of the period between 1865 and the turn of the century, a period that he knew very well and had taught for years. Jones's second major book written in retirement, *The Age of Energy: Varieties of American Experience, 1865–1915* (1971), would some twenty-five years after his debate with Spiller vindicate his stand. In the 1940s Jones referred to the last decades of the nineteenth century as the American Silver Age. He was thinking of William Jennings Bryan's famous Cross of Gold speech, but in the back of his mind there was also an allusion to the pre-Imperial Silver Age of Roman poetry. What disturbed Jones was the way this period in the American historical imagination had become glued to the pejorative label *The Gilded Age*. The corruption of the age, perpetuated in the title of Mark Twain's novel of social criticism, had totalized it in its worst image. What was literary history for, if it did not correct such misconceptions? Jones felt strongly that the Silver Age was an intellectual and social incubator of great significance in the maturation of American culture. He summarized his ideas in a dense little note to Spiller: "American Silver Age (1865–1890): Cosmopolitanism vs. realism; sociological and economic forces override politics and philosophy; democratizing of literature as culture becomes pedagogical."[21]

The principal reason Jones was so upset about the slighting of the Silver Age had much to do with his conviction that in this period America had found a way to produce a credible and even vital popular culture. We shall see later, in a closer look at *The Age of Energy* in

21. Vanderbilt, *American Literature and the Academy*, 436.

Chapter 7, how Jones made his case. Jones's conviction that a healthy popular culture would do much to keep America on its Jeffersonian course had a profound influence on one of our most influential literary historians, Roy Harvey Pearce.

In the early 1960s, before Jones had reissued his *Theory of American Literature* postscript of 1965, Pearce wrote two essays for *College English,* which he later included in his manifesto *Historicism Once More,* published in 1969. These essays touched on the relationship between criticism and literature and between literature and society, problems that Jones had addressed in 1948:

> The history of these modes (literary history and criticism) from the beginning almost to our own time is dealt with at large in Howard Mumford Jones's *Theory of American Literature.* I have been encouraged to say what I have to say by Professor Jones's fine study; yet, of course, I want to go a little further than he does. I want to go into the consequences for our criticism, especially the recent consequences, of the fact that literature has never had a clearly institutionalized status in our culture.

Pearce recognized that New Criticism freed literature from politics and "genteel tradition oriented literary historians and positivistic reductionists," but, he wrote, it went too far in rejecting history outright and in ignoring "the 'Americanization' of literature as an institution."[22] He gave Matthiessen a great deal of credit for combining formalism and historicism in a manner that provided a model for the articulation of literary sensibility in a truly American context. Pearce praised Saul Bellow's *Adventures of Augie March* as a work that took a "marginal" protagonist to the center of a fictional "world" created by Bellow's ear for the language and his grasp of the cultural moment. Bellow had what Melville called our "apprehension of the absolute condition of present things." In the second essay, which predated "Literature, History, and Humanism" but was printed after it in *Historicism Once More,* Pearce fleshed out what he felt must prevail in our society if the "condition of present things" is to play a significant role in American literary art. It is here that he picked up the baton that Jones dropped with portentous pronouncement on the last page of the 1948 edition of his *Theory of American Literature.*

To avoid the swamp of mass culture, elitist culture must forge an

22. *Historicism Once More: Problems and Occasions for the American Scholar,* 52–53.

alliance with popular culture. Popular culture must be helped to produce an art that will not lend itself to mass media exploitation and dilution: "I think," wrote Pearce, "that just as the shift from a painting by Kandinsky, to a monumental building by Gropius, to a Tech-Built house is evidence of a vital relation between elite and popular art, so such a relation exists (and can exist) for our songs and stories."[23] Pearce seemed to have worked his way back from elitist humanism to the discovery of a cultural humanism that can flourish in democratic accommodation between elitist and popular or folk culture.

For Jones, however, "the condition of present things" had always provided a context for his spiritual and intellectual growth; he could not bring himself to believe in any serious gap between folk or popular and elitist culture. From his midwestern childhood to his early academic wanderings across the nation, he had imbibed the full range of American possibility, and the liberating power of great ideas and art was forever mirrored in the epic promise of the America of his youth. Just as Beethoven, whom Jones classed with Goethe and Shakespeare as the greatest of geniuses, adapted the folk melodies of the Vienna woods to his symphonic works, Jones's breadth of learning was constantly enriched by the curious, often trivial, workings of the ordinary world around him. He wanted nothing to do with art that did not have a sense of its connection to the world of human experience; but then again he never found art or ideas that were not culturally joined.

We recall his sense of the greatest conundrum facing the literary historian. Should he be "encyclopedic or selective"? Jones never found it reasonable to make a clear choice. His passion for information made him appear a pedant to some of his students, and yet the best of them often found his learning infinitely suggestive and were encouraged by his example not to fear the immensity of what a humanist is expected to know. As for his writing, it is almost always supple and clear, and it carries the burden of its subject with grace and wit. The truth is that Jones derived confidence from the "encyclopedic" imperative; the more he knew, the surer was his "selectivity." If he never solved the problem of where the historian ends and the critic begins, he certainly had the historian's sense of shoring up the background and the critic's flair for

23. Ibid., 89.

taking the foreground in bold strides. Wesley Morris sums up exactly the kind of cultural criticism that Jones achieved: "I would claim that the historicist's view of literature offers nothing less than a corroboration of the freedom of human creativity within the bounds of historical meaning."[24]

24. *Toward a New Historicism,* 216. In a later work, imbued with postmodern ideas, Morris answers the question as to whether history had to be "encyclopedic or selective," a question that, as we have seen, he borrowed from Jones. Variations of both extremes, he now suggests, are at work at all times. In an indirect tribute to Jones's lifelong difficulties with the differences between Romanticism and rationalism, Morris writes, "Neither a pure romanticism nor a pure classicism is adequate to a fully developed hermeneutics" *(Friday's Footprint: Structuralism and the Articulated Text,* 220).

4

Types and Tropes

The modern critic of culture must have what Lionel Trilling called an appreciation for "complexity." In Trilling's case this resulted in a convoluted liberalism that constantly put him in a defensive position with the Left and could cause awkward moments when conservatives resisted his praise. Robert Frost, for example, was made truly uncomfortable with Trilling's readiness to crown him with the laurels of a Sophoclean tragic poet.[1] Howard Mumford Jones never commanded quite so great an audience as Trilling, but, like Trilling, he too thought in a broad spectrum—historical, philosophical, political, critical—and, again like Trilling, Jones did not permit himself the luxury of rationalizing the complexities of culture in all-embracing theories. Jones was less the critic but more the scholar than Trilling and perhaps even more sensitive to the risks of reductionism. In his day New Criticism reduced literary texts to acts of language to interpret their organic cohesion. At the time of his death, deconstruction was reducing literary texts to acts of language to *undermine* their cohesion. In recent years New Historicists have blurred the distinction between texts and history in ways that often reduce history to texts.

1. Stanley Burnshaw, *Robert Frost Himself*, 101–8.

Hayden White, not one of the New Historicists but a postmodern historian influenced by Derrida's philosophy of language, published *Tropics of Discourse* in 1978, two years before Jones died. Jones did not know White's book. From what I have been able to gather from Jones's students and colleagues, "historiography," when used at all by his generation, was a concept identified primarily with ideas of history itself rather than rhetorical strategies. White's central thesis, on the other hand, argues that the language and styles used by historians, rather than their command of facts and philosophical inclinations, will determine what their texts convey *as history;* the discourse itself is the true subject. This is somewhat reminiscent of W. K. Wimsatt's influential essay on the nature of Romantic imagery in *The Verbal Icon* (1954). Wimsatt suggested that in Romantic poetry the "vehicle" often becomes the "tenor." What Wimsatt saw as a unique moment in the history of poetics, White, under the influence of poststructuralist theory, expanded to a rhetorical theory crucial for all forms of historical narrative: "The discourse is intended to *constitute* the ground whereon to decide *what shall count as a fact* in matters under consideration and to determine what *mode of comprehension* is best suited to the understanding of the facts thus constituted."[2]

All his life Jones was intensely aware of the performatory dimension in successful discourse. In a letter to Walter B. Rideout, he had remarked as early as 1958 that modern poets are as "rhetorical" as the Victorians whom they delight to ridicule. No literary mind could ignore the tug of language that connects rhetoric to thought. Hayden White, however, insists that the tropical nature of discourse is such that it determines not only the style but the actual substance of what a writer manages to mean. For Jones also there is something inevitable in the coming together of ideas and rhetoric, but the meeting is not the result of any determinisms in discourse; it *is* the result of the writer's imagination and skill in manipulating the rhetorical possibilities of the subject. The best rhetoric is that which has emerged from the fiercest struggle with intractable knowledge. As Jones said of his ideal literary historians, "They are so steeped in knowledge, they have passed beyond particulars into philosophy; they live, as it were, double lives—one in the present tense, and one . . . in that portion of the human story that has claimed and riveted their attention for so long,

2. *Tropics of Discourse: Essays in Cultural Criticism,* 3.

they cannot exist without expressing in orderly prose its greatness and importance."[3]

Perhaps Jones would have conceded to White that history is fated to be narrative, but one wonders if this is not as much a fact of life as a fact of history, or for that matter the rhetorical face of history. That narrative shares with other tropes an essentially alogical character is certainly true, but tropical discourse is not our only way of conceptualizing alogical experience. Simon Schama has argued that there is an empirical thrust to seeing history as narrative because so many historical figures conceive of themselves as heroes of narrative. Tzvetan Todorov has suggested that narrative is so basic to our mental sense of order that it transcends linguistic categorization. Roland Barthes puts it even more strongly: "Caring nothing for the division between good and bad literature, narrative is international, trans-historical, transcultural; it is simply there, like life itself."[4]

Jones's three major works (*O Strange New World,* 1964; *The Age of Energy,* 1971; *Revolution and Romanticism,* 1974) are the fruit of a lifetime of study and teaching, all of them written in his seventies and the last published when he was eighty-two. He had every right to enjoy himself in a loose and even rambling narrative line, but "selectivity" could not defer to "encyclopedic" temptation; he had to keep his agon, or dialectic, between reason and feeling in focus. Narrative rules, but only because Jones found it the best instrument to convey his command of a wide variety of subjects lucidly and often in sparkling prose. The subject shines through his prose, not the rhetoric through the subject. Whenever his rhetoric was on display, he invariably ironized it in order to give his subject a sharper profile. He was in command of the rhetoric; the rhetoric was not in command of him. When he reflected on the first two books of his trilogy in his *Autobiography,* he noted simply, "On rereading *The Age of Energy,* I find it a better organized book than *O Strange New World* but one which is unfortunately written in denser prose."[5]

3. "The old dodo in me speaking observes with profound surprise how markedly rhetorical the moderns are. They are in the main afraid to say something directly. . . . They are as verbose and roundabout and full of orotund sound and orotund vocables as the Victorians, whom they abuse" (HMJ to Walter Rideout, June 6, 1958, Walter Rideout's personal papers); "The Nature of Literary History," in *Violence and Reason,* 177–78.

4. "Introduction to the Structural Analysis of Narratives," in *Image-Music-Text,* 79.

5. *Autobiography,* 269.

At the time of his retirement, Jones recalled with nostalgia the days when writing was a craft that one attempted to master through incessant practice, like learning the piano, and when "'to write' was a transitive verb—in the sense that one wrote stories, or verse, or *something.*" Hayden White's contention that "every discourse is always as much about discourse itself as it is about the objects that make up its subject matter" would have struck Jones as a tautology—a rhetorical observation that should submit to logical correction. And I suspect that he would also have questioned White's belief that the "self-critical" or "ironical" wielder of discourse was simply illustrating the inability of discourse "to be governed by logic alone." Perhaps not by "logic alone," but certainly more often than not with logic! Plato forever joined irony and reason in the very discourse of Socrates' dialogues. White's excessive interest in discourse as a "process of understanding" more identified with "meditation and consciousness" than with expository and analytical clarification would, I suspect, have finally caused Jones's hackles to rise in indignation at the reduction of the reflexiveness of discourse to a state of rumination closer to the unconscious than the conscious mind. For him all of this would be seen as further evidence of the "uncritical acceptance of a shallow doctrine of human nature as fundamentally irrational."[6]

Hayden White's historiographical prioritizing of figurative language and its closeness to the "strategies" of the "unconscious" is now shared by ethical philosophers like Richard Rorty who have made similar claims for the "contingency" of all thought: "Freud thus helps us to take seriously the possibility that there is no central faculty, no central self, called 'reason' . . . . The Platonic and Kantian idea of rationality centers around the idea that we need to bring particular actions under general principles to be moral. Freud suggests that we need to return to the particular." Finally, however, Rorty retreats from seeing in figurative language a substitute for reason: "A language which was 'all metaphor' would be a language which had no use, hence not a language but just babble. For even if we agree that languages are not media of representation or expression, they will remain media of communication, tools for social interaction, ways of tying oneself up with other human beings."[7]

6. "Be Obscure, Clearly"; White, *Tropics of Discourse,* 3, 4; HMJ, "A Farewell to the English Department," in *Violence and Reason,* 56.

7. *Contingency, Irony, and Solidarity,* 33, 41.

Jones would have taken solace in Rorty's second thoughts. He himself had too much to accomplish to wallow in the free association of his metaphors, to indulge in contingency at the expense of continuity. The enormity of his subject forced him to be nimble, quick, and lucid. Any soft-mindedness or lack of integrity that might tempt him to drift within his range of knowledge could be his undoing. Precisely because he was "Mr. Memory" and knew more "particulars" than others, the need to generalize with power was all the greater. He had to be arresting, witty, pithy, and always interesting. His subject would drown him in turgid pedantry if he gave it half a chance. And the vision at the heart of everything he wrote demanded intelligibility. He believed that literary culture told a democratic "story" in America, and it would run counter to the spirit of that culture to write about it in language that was not accessible to the average educated citizen. Although he admired Matthew Arnold's cosmopolitan agenda for "culture," Jones balked at his insensitivity to democratic feelings: "And what were the *Discourses in America*? I shall confine myself to the first lecture he gave. Entitled 'Numbers,' this was originally delivered in New York City, and is as pretty a little piece of antidemocratic propaganda as you can possibly find, even today."[8]

In *O Strange New World* not only was Jones's subject vast—the interplay between the Old and New Worlds in the three hundred years between the earliest explorations and the establishment of the nation—but it was also a subject so identified with contradiction and polarity that to strive for a synthesis that could either explain or resolve the stubbornly dichotomous evidence seemed quixotic. Jackson Turner's famous theory on the role of the frontier had attempted to free American history from the confusions surrounding its origins and destiny. To be European, or not to be—that was the nagging question that dogged thought in America and refused to yield to the authority of either traditional American society on the East Coast or the new immigration from all the corners of Europe. Turner transformed the receding western frontier into a magnet, and the old polarity (Ameri-

8. "American Literature and the Melting Pot," in *Ideas in America,* 196. The lecture, originally given at Southern Methodist University in 1941, has particular relevance to the multicultural agenda of today. Jones debunks the notion that America was ever a bastion of Anglo-Saxon culture by carefully tracing statistics in immigration and demography.

can-European) yielded to his resetting of the compass. The "frontier" now reshaped whatever came its way, American or European.

Jones had come from the "west" and experienced its early presumptions to cultural integrity, but in his thinking about prenational America he was persuaded that, although "New" and "Old" were indeed different worlds, the balance of authority leaned in the direction of Europe. True enough, it was only a leaning. One could not simply defer to a Jamesian veneration for the European principle; nor could one entirely share the comic disdain of things European in Mark Twain's travel sketches. Jones concluded: "The Old World projected into the New a rich, complex, and contradictory set of habits, forces, practices, values, and presuppositions; and the New World accepted, modified, or rejected these or fused them with inventions of their own." This is not much of a synthesis of the dialectical tension between European and American culture, but then Jones never promised to provide a thesis that would resolve this question. Instead, his purpose was to flesh out the historical evidence for the uniqueness of both European and American ideas in the formation of what eventually became our national culture. To do this Jones, citing the English legal historian Frederic William Maitland, assigned himself the task of gathering "not what happened but what people thought or said about what happened." Obviously, Jones did not mean the secondary sources of his own day. He planned "to find out what people thought or said or imagined about the New World and about the republic of the west" at the time certain "facts" were thought to have occurred.[9]

It could be argued that in taking this view of the historian's task, Jones is assuming a theoretical position more radical than Hayden White's tropism. Jones is suggesting that history itself, not merely historiography, is composed largely of the facts that have been written or inscribed in discourse, not necessarily the facts that are supposed to have happened. As the old story about the elephant and the several blind men well illustrates, empiricism has no great respect for the reliability of narrative. Once the narrative voice begins, it and all listeners (or readers) are at the mercy of the narrator's memory, bias, and prose. There is no need to raise the indeterminacy of language or the determinism of tropes rising from the unconscious to establish the fact that history is finally historiography. It may be that one of the

9. "Preface," in *O Strange New World,* vii–viii.

reasons Jones and his generation did not ponder the problems of historiography was that no clearer understanding of the truth of history could be achieved by scrutinizing its rhetorical procedures in the abstract. Whatever could be learned about the language of history in this way could not finally question or affirm the empirical validity of what the language recorded. The best that Jones could do was to adjust his focus and avoid the repetition of previously worked subjects and points of view:

> The political history of the colonies and of the United States has been sufficiently written about and so, I think, has its religious history, at least in these earlier epochs, nor do we lack histories of American Literature. I have therefore touched upon these great themes but incidentally and have preferred to take what I hope is an imaginative look at other great trends or components in the transit of civilization across the Atlantic.[10]

Although Jones gives himself ironic credit for "originality of synthesis" in the preface to *O Strange New World,* chapter headings exude binary and chiasmic playfulness: "The Image of the New World" is followed by "The Anti-Image"; "Renaissance Man in America" crosses with "The Colonial Idea in England"; "The Radical Republic" transposes into "Republican Culture." We remember that Jones was an actor and director in his youth. He saw the text as a stage, and he was very much aware of all exits and entrances, of rising and falling action, and, most of all, of the importance of conflict. The conflict between the "Old" and "New" worlds is never truly resolved, but the entrances and exits keep the reader going through revolving scenes with a sense of expectation. Will the "strange" new world become a "brave" one after all? This arrested or thwarted synthesis is not an indication of what Paul de Man calls "blindness" as "insight"; nor is it what J. Hillis Miller might designate as the contradiction that unravels the work. It *is* a conscious form of scholarly good humor by a literary and cultural historian who takes intellectual pleasure in sharing the organizational burden of his project by underscoring the binary tension of his subject.

Good contrasts usually arise from a contemplation of things essentially alike, good comparisons from a contemplation of things fundamentally different. Jones thought of himself as a defender of rhetorical craft ("Writing is no longer a difficult craft, the English language is no

10. Ibid., vii.

longer an exquisite tool of accuracy") in an age that confused craft with art ("Writing has become therapy, a form of self-expression. Its mandate is no longer to communicate but to create"). Jones blew hot and cold on the expressive aesthetic of Romantic and post-Romantic thought, which is central to Hayden White's historiographical determinism. White identifies the "representation of opposites" as "the third phase of discursive representation," which is preceded by an intricate "prerational progress defined by Freud and Piaget."[11] For Jones, however, the writing of history could not be, finally, the same thing as writing poetry. Discursive thought must be identified primarily with rational process; no matter what in the way of impression or emotion feeds the thoughts of the historian, he does not get involved in a "cognitive process" until he has reached deduction. Jones reverses White's paradigm by beginning with contrast ("opposition") and then, with characteristic gusto, coursing through various tropes.

All this is illustrated in the following magisterial paragraph in chapter 6 of *O Strange New World* ("The Useful and the Good"), where Jones sets out to contrast the southern and northern Renaissance in Europe:

> After the Renaissance of the South, the Renaissance of the North, which pursues analogous aims but bears the Reformation in its bosom. The bright colors of the Mediterranean world, the chiaroscuro of brilliance and blackness that is Spain and Italy, the half-African energy and languor of Portugal fill the vision for a time, then make way for the soberer cultures, the more familiar products, the temperate landscapes of northern France, the Low Countries, the Germanies, and the British Isles. To the subtle, half-pagan, and wholly sensuous charm of Botticelli, Leonardo, Correggio, and the Venetians succeed Dürer, who had reached only his maturity when Columbus sailed; Holbein, who was twenty when Luther affixed his ninety-five theses to the church door in Wittenberg; and, by and by, Frans Hals, Rubens, and Rembrandt. On the one side the *terribilita* of Michelangelo; on the other the "Melancholia" of Dürer, which, created in 1514, followed the completion of the central vault of the Sistine Chapel ceiling by four years. In the Renaissance of the South mythological subjects express a nostalgic idealism, as if the direct heirs of the antique world were imaginatively returning upon their birthright; but the same themes in the North, painted by Rubens or, more rarely, by Rembrandt, exist, so to speak, in present time and are clothed in present flesh—the warriors vigorous and immense, modeled on the men who resisted Alba, the women less nude

11. *Tropics of Discourse*, 1–7.

> than unclad, so that we may see what good food and drink produce in beautiful plumpness. Portraits in the South mirror personality; in the North they express character. Pictures by Gerard Douw, de Hooch, Vermeer, and Maes lovingly insist upon tangible things in a bourgeois universe as the fading glories of Venice yield to the splendor of Antwerp, that "flower of the world," which, when it vacates pride of place, gives way not to Genoa, Cadiz, Seville, or Lisbon but to Amsterdam. In vain does Charles V, perhaps the last monarch to believe in universal empire, struggle to restore a lost medieval unity, in vain does Philip II endeavor to stamp out heresy; the tough Protestant spirit overcomes him, the mercantile navies of the North check and turn back, as it were, the chivalry of the South. Feudalism retreats eastward to the plains beyond the Elbe; in the Low Countries, in England, in France, even in Scandinavia the merchant class comes more and more to determine policy. The trade of the North is in necessities, and the Mediterranean triad of olive oil, wine, and "corn" seems exotic to countries trafficking in salt fish, lumber, woolens and naval stores. The movement of culture is from Francis I to Colbert, from Sir Thomas More to Bacon, from Paracelsus, who, said his enemies, died drunk, to William Gilbert, the discoverer of the earth's magnetism, and William Harvey, the discoverer of the circulation of the blood.[12]

The heart of the deduction that enables Jones to conceive one "Renaissance" in opposition to the other, to see them in contrast rather than comparatively, is positioned neatly in the center of the paragraph: "Portraits in the South mirror personality; in the North they express character." Some late twentieth-century readers may hear overtones of Anglo-Saxon racism in this sentence, but they should read his essays "American Literature and the Melting Pot" and "Tribalism" in *Ideas in America*. The true subtext here is the contrast between Hebraism and Hellenism, a dialectic that Matthew Arnold took from Heinrich Heine—two poet-critics important to Jones. He came eventually to identify the tension between personality and character as a clue to solving the puzzle of American culture: how could a society committed to Puritanical gloom deal with its great longing for the sunshine of pleasure?[13]

12. *O Strange New World*, 194–95.

13. In *The Pursuit of Happiness* (1952), Jones deals more directly than anywhere else with this question. Max Lerner, *America as a Civilization: Life and Thought in the United States Today*, 693, summarizes Jones's thesis: "[HMJ] has traced the web of meaning in the concept of the 'pursuit of happiness.' . . . One phase came from . . . classical writers, who saw happiness (as Jefferson himself saw it) as a gracious way of life led by landed gentry or farmers, with leisure . . . for books . . . science, the arts, and Nature. The second came from the Puritan idea of obeying God's laws and having a store of worldly

Driven by this intensely perceived idea, which he meditated through his broad knowledge of Western culture, Jones proceeded to play with it tropologically in this paragraph. The opening fragment salutes common historical knowledge: the Reformation is a northern phenomenon. The first true sentence is long but not complex; it compounds information by balancing and interweaving nominatives in an intricate series. As the paragraph develops, great passages from Ruskin and Pater come to mind and by association seem to lend a majestic surge to Jones's prose. A growing density of names, places, and things swarms over the page and strains at the confines of the paragraph, but the reader is dazzled by the way these details sparkle on Jones's palette. The "bright colors of the Mediterranean world" yield to the "beautiful plumpness" of Rembrandt's nudes. Largely metonymic, Jones's blend of figure and fact enables him to be faithful to the fragmentary nature of historical evidence without losing faith in its intelligibility. For Jones, metonymy is a way of demonstrating how what appears fragmentary is actually an allegory for a plenitude yet to be revealed. Literature, art, music, commerce, society, government, religion, landscape—all become metonymies, parts of a culture for which they are all metaphors. Although all of this figuration provides little in the way of teleological comfort, it does offer intellectual light. And the binary discoveries sweep up the metonymies into classifications that often energize new points of view, new possibilities of thinking.

Jones's delight in tropes is grounded in his sense of their dramatic usefulness, their power to make concrete what he has already deduced in the abstract. Longinus too had an idea of the sublime before he cataloged its rhetorical and figurative variety. Today, however, theorists of language tend to side with Hayden White's view that the tropes come first. White credits Kenneth Burke, as do many others, with having initiated a psychological progress toward increasingly sophisticated cognition by placing the "master tropes" (metaphor, metonymy, synecdoche, and irony) at the head of the class. To begin with tropes is to make Freud's unconscious the source of all thought, an idea possible only if the repression barrier that Freud himself, and Lacan even more stringently, placed between the unconscious and conscious mind is seen as the sentry controlling everything from the

goods to show for it. This in turn was linked with . . . the nineteenth century . . . idea of material success."

solving of equations to the choice of one's supper.[14] This does happen to be the view of William Blake, but it is not entirely appropriate for the average day's intellection—nor is it a reliable model for expository history. Even in literature, figures rarely generate feelings unless a discursive context is in place; it is often vaguely present, but it is there. We cannot feel the power of F. Scott Fitzgerald's tropical equation of Daisy Buchanan's voice with "money" without the contextualizing support provided by the typologies of genre (romance and/or novel of manners), ethics (social criticism), and social and literary history (Jazz Age; Fitzgerald's love affair with the rich).

Hayden White himself, in his influential first book, *Metahistory: The Historical Imagination in Nineteenth-Century Europe* (1973), praised by René Wellek as "a great achievement . . . the only substantial American contribution to the history of historiography," had grounded his historiographical classifications in a typology based on traditional literary genres rather than linguistically defined tropes. He had remembered the revolutionary use of generic classification in Northrop Frye's *Anatomy of Criticism* (1957) and adapted it for his own historiographical map: Michelet is identified with romance, Ranke with comedy, Tocqueville with tragedy, and Burckhardt with satire. White, however, goes on to classify the more recent "modern" philosophers of history as writing in the "metonymical mode" (Marx), in the "metaphorical mode" (Nietzsche), and in the "ironic mode" (Croce). White casts his paradigm in an alloy of rhetorical and historical determinism; historiography is both psychologized ("prerational progress defined by Freud and Piaget") and, in the Heideggerian fashion of interweaving language and being, ontologized.[15] Furthermore, in perceiving the movement of typology to tropology as historical trend, White seems to be giving it the dialectical authority of Hegelian progression; tropological discourse, in its Freudian context, is not exactly in tune with the rationalism implicit in Hegel's idea of the Spirit of History. Not only would Jones have raised an eyebrow over the implicit irrational-

14. White, *Tropics of Discourse*, 5; Françoise Meltzer, "Unconscious," 156.

15. René Wellek, "The Content of the Form. Narrative Discourse and Historical Representation, a Review," 334. Thirty-five years ago Georg Lukács identified in modern literature the philological and rhetorical characteristics that today dominate literary theory and historiography: "The ontology of *Geworfenheit* [Heidegger] makes a true typology impossible; it is replaced by an abstract polarity of the eccentric and the socially average" ("The Ideology of Modernism," 604).

izing of Hegel, but he also would have questioned an alliance of rhetoric, psychology, and ontology that minimized the historical connection between rhetoric and literature. Aristotle and Longinus look almost exclusively at literary texts for their rhetorical models, and Kenneth Burke, whom others besides White have celebrated as the father of modern tropology, was generically identified with "dramatistic" values and was therefore rooted in literary typology.

When Jacques Derrida notes that "every text participates in one or several genres; there is no genreless text; there is always a genre and genres, yet such participation never amounts to belonging," he is forcing genre under a tropological umbrella; he is suggesting that the "traces" and "aporia" of typological engagement involve the same level of indeterminacy as tropes in lexical and rhetorical context. It is certainly true that genres have been blending and overlapping since, and even before, the debates on the relative merits of tragedy, comedy, epic, and lyric in the Renaissance. In Milton at least three of these forms blended in *Paradise Lost* and *Samson Agonistes.* The modern novel is nothing other than a medley of all four. In recent decades nonliterary forms, which recall the achievements of Swift and Carlyle, have more than kept pace with the ingenuity of the novel for blending genres:

> Scientific discussions looking like belles lettres "morceaux" (Lewis Thomas, Loren Eisley), baroque fantasies presented as deadpan empirical observations (Borges, Barthelme), histories that consist of equations and tables of law court testimony (Fogel and Engerman, LeRoi Ladurie), documentaries that read like true confessions (Mailer), parables posing as ethnographies (Casteneda), theoretical treaties set out as travelogues (Lévi-Strauss), Nabokov's *Pale Fire,* that impossible object made of poetry and fiction, footnotes and images from the clinic, seems very much of the time: one waits only for quantum theory in verse or biography in algebra.[16]

The shifts, however, in ideas and taste that have contributed to tampering with genres cannot be abstracted to the point where we think of them merely as tropologically induced forces. Despite all the work done on American literary metaphors from Harry Levin to Leo Marx from the 1940s to the 1960s, few would argue that Richard

16. Jacques Derrida's remarks come from "The Law of Genre," *Gylph* 7 (Spring 1980); rept. *Critical Inquiry* (Autumn 1980): 55–81. They are quoted by Marjorie Perloff in her "Introduction," in *Postmodern Genres,* ed. Marjorie Perloff (Norman: Oklahoma University Press, 1991), 4. Clifford Geertz's already famous purple passage is cited by Ralph Cohen, "Do Postmodern Genres Exist?" in the same volume, 15.

Chase's important distinction between the novel and the romance, and the importance of the latter as a typological guide to American fiction, rested primarily on the matter of rhetorical figures. Even a champion of metaphor like John Crowe Ransom relied heavily on genre in making his case for the uniqueness of Hardy's poems: "They are like quick but sure little dramas; or in their folkways they make us think of epics in miniature. But if we look for the genre which seems most likely to describe them we may call them fables."[17]

Certainly the complexity of interweaving genres invites descriptive criticism. Nevertheless, despite the ingenuity of this kind of inquiry, it often has a scholastic ring and tends to atomize the text. Generic quilting reduces generic or typological difference to a problem in description similar to that posed by tropical "différance." The difficulty with this kind of reductionism is that, as suggested above, it obscures some extremely important distinctions that hierarchical genre theory was able to keep in sharp focus.

When Aristotle argued that tragedy is a "higher . . . mode of imitation than epic," he began by dismissing shallow notions about the "histrionic" context of tragedy. He did this evidently to emphasize the fact that his hierarchical criteria had nothing to do with superficial notions of social superiority based on prejudices about who does and who does not enjoy the exaggerated "gestures" of theatrical performance. After all, he wrote, "gesticulation may be equally overdone in epic recitation" (readers will recall Socrates bating Ion in the dialogue that bears his name). Aristotle's dismissal of socio-affective criteria as significant factors in the determination of generic hierarchy stands in striking contradiction to contemporary wisdom, which is obsessed with the elitist implications of any and all suggestions of hierarchy. M. H. Abrams is certainly not a devotee of postmodern anti-elitism, but even he seems to dismiss traditional generic hierarchy as too closely related to social distinctions to be taken seriously in the contemporary world. It is not surprising that today's theorists, wary of any elitist associations, keep a strategic distance: "Modern genre theory . . . tends to be descriptive and to avoid any overt assumptions about generic hierarchies."[18]

17. "Introduction" to *Selected Poems of Thomas Hardy,* x.

18. M. H. Abrams, *Glossary of Literary Terms,* 73; Roger Fowler, ed., *Dictionary of Modern Literary Terms,* 104.

For Aristotle hierarchy was textual, not social. In remarkable anticipation of postmodern grounding in the text—not to mention Barthean "écriture" and all shades of reader-response theory—Aristotle continued to make his case for the ascendancy of tragedy over epic in the following passage:

> Tragedy like Epic poetry produces its effect even without action [performance]; it reveals its power by mere reading. If, then, in all other respects it is superior, this fault [histrionic gesture], we say, is not inherent in it. And superior it is, because it has all the epic elements . . . and these produce the most vivid of pleasures. Further, it has vividness of impression in reading as well as in representation. Moreover, the art attains its end within narrower limits; for the concentrated effect is more pleasurable than one which is spread over a long time and so diluted. What, for example, would be the effect of the Oedipus of Sophocles, if it were cast into a form as long as the Iliad? Once more, the Epic imitation has less unity; as is shown by this, that any Epic poem will furnish subjects for several tragedies.[19]

So neatly does Aristotle subsume the paradox that tragedy can include all the strategies and tropes of epic and nevertheless meet the aesthetic requirement of unity to a far greater degree than epic that we may have forgotten how much trouble the same problem of balancing "encyclopedic" range and "selectivity" posed for Howard Mumford Jones as literary and cultural historian. Of course, Aristotle's insistence that poetry was more "philosophical" than history may partly explain history's struggle to keep pace. For all of Jones's distaste for the substitution of "creativity" for "communication" in contemporary exposition (which he saw as the irrationalizing of discourse), there was enough of the rhapsode in him to know that he had to be something of a poet to be a philosophical historian. Just as Plato's Ion felt that Homer was his forte, Jones was instinctively attracted to epic. To be a successful narrative historian—and Herodotus and Thucydides came to the same conclusion—one had to sacrifice the unity of tragedy for what Aristotle himself maintained was an undeniable advantage in epic: "Owing to the narrative form, many events simultaneously transacted can be presented; and these, if relevant to the subject, add mass and dignity to the poem."[20]

19. Aristotle, *Poetics,* XXVI, in Walter Jackson Bate, ed., *Criticism: The Major Texts,* 38.
20. Ibid., XXIV, 35.

5

The Epic Imperative

Jones's attraction to epic for its plenitude and its tolerance of irresolution and conflict puts him at odds with Hegel, the father of modern historiography. Hayden White's brilliant explication of Hegel begins by noting his understanding of the historian's necessary involvement with poetic expression: "Like Thucydides, the historian must remain closer to the poetic mode of apprehension, closer to Metaphorical identification of his object, but at the same time be more self-critical, more aware of the modalities of comprehension used to transform a poetic insight into the content of a more rational knowledge." It is the historian's need to be "self-critical" that moves him away from epic and toward tragedy and comedy. In other words, according to Hegel, the historian's subtle contract with poetic modes moves him toward an idea of the hierarchy of genres similar to Aristotle's. "The content of Tragic action, Hegel wrote, is the same as that of history: we *apprehend* it immediately in the aims of tragic characters, but *comprehend* it fully only as 'the world of those forces which carry in themselves their own justification, and are realized substantively in the volitional activity of mankind.'" Tragedy is a more reliable model for the historian than epic because it "takes not conflict itself as its object (as the Epic tends to do), but rather that condition of resolution, in which both the hero and the common life are transformed, which lies on the other side of this conflict." Nevertheless, it is comedy that has the last word. White sums up Hegel's idea of history by alluding to the implications of his metaphysics: "Thus, the whole series of Pathetic, Epic, and Tragic Dramas contained in the historical record are sublimated into a Drama of essentially Comic significance, a human Comedy, a theodicy which is a justification not so much of the ways of God to man as of man's own ways to himself." Jones was highly conscious of Hegel's idea of the ironic undertow to all of history, and he captured its tone in his translation of Heine's last stanza of the ninth section of the second cycle of "The North Sea," entitled "In Haven":

Thou worthy Ratskeller-owner of Bremen,
See there—on the roofs of the houses, angels
Are sitting, and they're all drunk and they're singing;
The fiery sun there above us
Is only the crimsoning nose of a drunkard,
The nose of the Weltgeist;
And round the Weltgeist's crimson nose
Circles the world on a glorious drunk![1]

Aristotle placed comedy lower than tragedy because comedy depicts men worse than they are and tragedy depicts them better. That moral distinction was irrelevant to Hegel because the "panorama of sin and suffering" that is history can only be explained by moral reflection, not understood. Hegel's dismissal of the ethical criterion for an understanding of the true meaning of history is connected to his dismissal of epic "as an appropriate form of historiography . . . because it does not presuppose substantial change." Hegel seems to contradict himself when it comes to the suitability of epic as a form of emplotment for history. He chides it for being essentially frozen in mythic and archetypal expectations but nevertheless preoccupied with unresolved conflict. Hegel's quarrel with epic seems to be based largely on its appeal to what he called "Universal" and "Practical" history rather than "Critical" or "Conceptual." Hence epic encouraged the rush to unwarranted "typologies" of utilitarian purpose but prevented historians from doing rigorous thinking. Hayden White's gradual shift from typology to tropology in his historiography is based primarily

1. Hayden White, *Metahistory: The Historical Imagination in Nineteenth-Century Europe*, 92, 95, 122; HMJ, ed. and trans., *Heine's Poem: The North Sea*, 120.

on the assumption that the blurred state of genres in modern discourse is proof of their unreliable taxonomy; on the other hand, tropes like metaphor and synecdoche, argues White, pursue language analytically and therefore realize the "Critical" and "Conceptual" tasks urged by Hegel. Hegel certainly questioned typologies in place, but he did not dismiss typology itself. What White, I believe, tends to ignore is that to denigrate typology does violence to reason itself. It may be that the dialectical fervor of Hegel's epistemology is partially responsible for separating modern thought from Hegel's own metaphysical grounding in reason. In addition, the influence of Freud has psychologized thought in the very act of rationalizing its nature. The turning away in modern thinkers from a general understanding of being (*Wesen*) to a sharply individualized or phenomenal grasp of being (*Sein*) has brought us to the point where irrationality and objectivity have become strange bedfellows.[2]

This is exactly the situation that Georg Lukács deplored in the 1950s (see above). Heidegger's *Faktizität* (facticity) or *Tatsätzlichkeit* (actuality) brackets rationality by endowing uniqueness and phenomenal experience with an immanence that somewhat casually ethicizes irrationality. From Nietzsche to Derrida, reason yields to what many different German thinkers already in the early years of this century were calling *das Neue Denken* (the new thinking).[3] Derrida's "indeterminacy" can be understood as the most recent affirmation of "the new thinking." In language, *das Einzelne* (the unique) is merely the result of slippery signification—an essentially irrational procedure. Significantly, Derrida no longer requires a metaphysics. Hegel would not have understood.

For all his awareness of the ironies of history, Howard Mumford Jones could not forsake his deeply ingrained sense of the connection between reason and ethics. "We have not achieved justice, virtue, and love on this planet, and perhaps we never shall, but to slacken in the search now, to abandon the age-long quest to followers of irrationality and fantastical theories—that is, indeed, the treason of the intellectuals."[4] Jones's faith in the ethical possibilities of literature, in the

2. White, *Metahistory*, 107, 93, 99.

3. Friedrich Georg Friedmann, *Von Cohen zu Benjamin: Zum Problem deutsch-jüdischer Existenz*, 52–69.

4. HMJ, *Violence and Reason*, 59. These remarks come from Jones's "Farewell to the English Department," an address given at a banquet of the Department of English at Harvard University on November 27, 1962, in honor of his retirement.

symbiosis of imagination and reason, identifies him with a view of the hierarchy of genres older than Hegel's and thus preemptive of late modern *and* postmodern perspectives.

"One of the notable departures of Renaissance criticism from Aristotle," wrote Walter Jackson Bate, "was to place the epic above tragedy as a poetic form."[5] In the eighteenth century the gradual discrediting of epic was due largely to its lack of objectivity and its commitment to heroic ideas of character; neither of these qualities spoke to the Enlightenment's grounding in rationalism. The bombast of heroic drama in Davenant and Dryden provides a clear example of how epic heroism had deteriorated into the very posturing that had caused Aristotle to dismiss gesticulation as a viable criterion for distinguishing between epic and tragedy in the first place. When Hegel called the novel the "bourgeois epic," he was not only expressing his contempt for the modern mind's tendency to aestheticize and fantasize *Geist,* but he was also emphasizing bourgeois nostalgia for a conventionally ethical idea of history. In the Renaissance, however, Platonic ideas of perfection outweighed Aristotelian dialectics. Castiglioni's courtier was a creature of perfect balance, at home in any place or time—in short, an epical emanation, a hero like Odysseus or Aeneas who moves from Calypso to Penelope and from Carthage to Rome without losing ethical power.

Heroics of this kind struck Hegel as nonsense. Despite the epic's mythic and narrative authority—its closeness to the dawn of history—it was rooted in fantasy and therefore useless to any philosophy of history. Shakespeare's tragicomic universe, on the other hand, spoke directly to Hegel's idea of *Zerrissenheit,* his sense of the antithetical drama of consciousness working itself out in history. Hamlet's enduring fascination in a post-Hegelian world comes largely from the fact that he cannot move from Gertrude to Ophelia; that, indeed, his inability to do so sparks the tragic action. He would not be Hamlet if Shakespeare had him move from a Calypso to a Penelope. When Shakespeare did imagine epic action of this kind, as in the Henriad, he had Prince Hal move from Falstaff to the king with an ethical awkwardness that troubles audiences to this day. Hamlet is far too mixed in his elements to be the sweet prince Horatio crowns at the end of the play. At the heart, then, of Hamlet's *Zerrissenheit* is the conflict in his conception between the epic and tragic hero. Shakespeare was in the

5. Walter Jackson Bate, ed., *Criticism: The Major Texts,* 95.

Renaissance, but not entirely of it; this, of course, is simply a more toughminded way of reinvoking Ben Jonson's praise. Sir Philip Sidney, on the other hand, cut from Castiglione's mold, was entirely of the Renaissance. For him it was patently clear that epic was more ethical than tragedy because it provided more heroical examples; in short, it was a clearer teacher of ethical behavior:

> Only let Aeneas be worn in the tablet of your memory, how he governeth himself in the ruin of his country, in the preserving his old father, and carrying away his religious ceremonies, in obeying the god's commandment to leave Dido, though not only all passionate kindness, but even the human consideration of virtuous gratefulness, would have craved other of him; how in storms, how in sports, how in war, how in peace, how a fugitive, how victorious, how besieged, how besieging, how to strangers, how to allies, how to enemies, how to his own; lastly, how in his inward self, and how in his outward government, and I think, in a mind not prejudiced with a prejudicating humour, he will be found in excellency fruitful.[6]

We remember how Jones in his controversial jeu d'esprit on *Hamlet* had resurrected Claudius from the background of the play and highlighted his political acumen, his healthy shrewdness—a prince of peace in contrast to his war-loving brother. That such a desirable king should also be a murderer spells a greater loss to Denmark than the passing of his brother, who, after all, had shed its blood recklessly. Jones's grasp of historical issues told him what the Renaissance audience would have felt was the richest pathos in the play, namely, a ruler of epic potential destroyed by lust and ambition, one of Sidney's "worthies" gone terribly wrong. No one will want to dispute that Shakespeare's great accomplishment in this play was to educate his audience to a pathos richer by far, the tragic condition of Hamlet. Shakespeare's achievement becomes Hegel's model, not only in his theory of tragedy but also, as Hayden White would have it, in his idea of historiography.

We come back now to my earlier assertion that Jones simply could not accept the modern return to the Aristotelian hierarchy of genres. Rooted in Hegel, modernism's dialectical thrust is continually thrown back into antithesis. The tension between the organic sweep of so much of Romantic and post-Romantic thought and its passion for immolation and shattered consciousness irritated Jones. Aristotelian

6. Cited in ibid.

unity and compression had been enlisted in the service of a symbolic art friendly to irrationalism; somehow formalism and madness had made a devil's pact to capture the tragic muse.

Jones had come to understand that in a post-Romantic culture the empirical world is itself a mixture of subject and object, but he would not credit the psychological structures of the subject, the powers of interpretation, with any kind of hierarchical authority greater than the hierarchical structures established by a rational and ethical evaluation of the object. Like Dr. Johnson, he was driven by the demands of sound generalization. He could not count the streaks of the tulip until he had an idea of the flower. He did not believe that his mind developed, according to the teachings of Freud and Piaget, from metaphor through metonymy to irony and classification—the mental journey charted by Hayden White as definitive of the rhetorical process in narrative history. He did not lead up to "oppositeness," as White says the mind moves; he started with it. We have already seen enough evidence of the binary cast of his mind. His natural bent to see and think in bilateral concepts was, as I have already suggested, characteristic of his strong identification with dramatic conflict. Jones found diversion in the theater throughout most of his professional academic life, but what developed in him as actor, director, lecturer, and raconteur found its fullest expression in his historiography. In the epic mode he found a dynamic field where he could do justice to the drama of history itself—a study in contrasts beyond theatricality.

The transcendentalist poet Jones Very announced in 1837 that the difficulty of producing epic literature in modern times was "proof of the progress of the soul, and of its approach to the state of being where its thought is action, its word power." Very's statement is very Hegelian, and in its equation of thought and power with something other than epic (that is, tragedy) seems to condemn epic to its most primitive model: action that is not thought, words that lack power. In his study of major American "epic novels" Leonard Lutwack notes, "No American epic hero fights to save a city, as is common in the Renaissance epic, but always to preserve some less sophisticated way of life."[7] His examples include *Moby Dick, The Octopus, The Grapes of Wrath,* and *For Whom the Bell Tolls.* Indeed, the epic strain in the American novel is

7. *The Epic Tradition and American Novels of the Twentieth Century,* 10–11. Lutwack gives *Essays and Poems,* 1839, as the source of Jones Very's remarks.

primitivistic and naturalistic; this is attributable largely to the fact that heroic action in American experience is rooted in struggle with overpowering forces in nature and society. From Cooper's wilderness to Farrell's slum, Darwinian forces dominate. In other words, the American epic novel circumvented the Hegelian objection to epic as a suitable model for historical consciousness by casting its dream of action in a primitive and mythic form that avoided objective confrontation of reality. When we add to this idea of the American novel as a primitive epic the long-held theory that the typical American fiction is more romance than novel, we have a two-pronged support of Hegel's famous dismissal of the modern novel as a "bourgeois epic."

Jones despaired repeatedly of the modern American novel because he felt it had lost its moorings in Jeffersonian egalitarianism and had sold out to Freudianism and various shades of social Darwinism. In a splenetic book, *Jeffersonianism and the American Novel,* published in 1966, Jones attacks modern writers for their betrayal of the heroic victory in reason at the time of the Revolution. For Jones the promise of American history lay precisely in its realization of the Hegelian dialectic in actual time. This explains his broad cultural frame of reference, the panoply of facts, and his endless critical attention to popular culture. *Geist* was phenomenological in America's story, but America had sacrificed its victory in reason to the irrationality of Hegel's divided self. The binary impulse in Jones's historiography transcended not only dramatic conflict but also tragic contradiction. He had gone beyond tragedy to a rediscovery of the Renaissance voice of historical immanence. Jones fought to "save" the "city" of Enlightenment thought. Since fiction had indirectly accepted Hegel's denigration of epic by settling for primitive realism and romance, Jones revived Renaissance epic in his historiography. In the preface to his epic poem *The Columbiad,* Joel Barlow emphasized that "the real object of the poem is to inculcate the love of rational liberty, and to discountenance the deleterious passion for violence and war." Charles and Mary Beard wrote "epic" histories of America that stressed its economic growth, but Jones's last three works resonate with an ebullience and expansionism that recall *The Lusiad* and Hakluyt while celebrating the same Enlightenment vision that had inspired Barlow.

Jones's faith in the Enlightenment's promise of liberty and social order runs counter to the position of modern thinkers who are concerned with both the historical "tragedy" of the Enlightenment's self-betrayal, as first explained by Horkheimer and Adorno, and the problem of belatedness. George Steiner, for example, connects the nostalgic return to "George Eliot and Tolstoy . . . to get things right again" with "appeals made . . . throughout the late seventeenth, the eighteenth and the nineteenth centuries to the epic lineage of Homer, Virgil, and Milton. It took centuries," continues Steiner, "for poets to realize that the high verse epic was a form gone inert, a genre whose social, stylistic, metaphysical presuppositions could not be artificially revived." It is true that the "verse epic" has not thrived in the twentieth century—although readers of William Carlos Williams and Ezra Pound might feel otherwise. In any case, if "verse epic" lasted from antiquity to the nineteenth century, is it not slightly premature to bury its "metaphysical presuppositions" in the twentieth? Furthermore, two pages after his dismissal of "verse epic" Steiner himself notes that the "structural complexity of a high modernist work like Ernst Bloch's *Das Prinzips Hoffnung*" requires the reader to rise to the challenge of coordinating the many parts of a complex discourse that combines "language experiment . . . imaginary memoir . . . ontological [thought]" *and* is "part epic voyage." Generic plenitude merely begs the question of hierarchy. Steiner's self-contradictory reliance on epic while dismissing its relevance to the modern world would suggest that Jones's stubborn retention of epic is not as naive as some might be inclined to believe.[8]

The Renaissance paradigm of epic replacing tragedy at the top of the literary hierarchy was deeply established in Jones's sensibility as a literary analogue to his Jeffersonian trust in the power of reason and ethics to educate the ordinary citizen to his heroic potential in a free society. His strong conviction that the American adventure represented an opportunity in actual historical time to realize a European cultural dream identified his imagination with the "epic spirit" as Tillyard describes it: "The epic writer must express the feelings of a large group of people living in or near his own time. . . . It is in this communal or choreic quality that epic most differs from tragedy. Tragedy cannot lack some imprint of its age, but its nature is to be time-

8. Max Horkheimer and Theodor W. Adorno, *Dialektik der Aufklärung: Philosophische Fragmente*, 1–7. This influential work was first published in the United States in 1944. Its authors, exiles from Hitler's Germany, believed that Nazism represented the nadir of the historical Enlightenment because education and science had been undermined by their own offspring—propaganda and technology—to enslave the masses. George Steiner, *Extraterritorial: Papers on Literature and the Language Revolution*, 164, 166.

less." We have seen how Jones wavered between the contemporary and the timeless in his evaluations of Poe and Melville. He would have agreed with Tillyard that "when the tragic intensity is included in the group consciousness of an age, when the narrowly timeless is combined with the variegatedly temporal . . . the epic attains its full growth." When Jones finally made his peace with the irrationalism implicit in Romantic will, he credited Romanticism and its epic-tragic emanation, "Faustian man," with establishing the irreducible authority of individual subjectivity: "The great, the unique contribution of romanticism to modernity is the insistence that every human being is a distinct and autonomous entity, whatever theories of education, or of sociology, or of political science, or of evolution say to the contrary. . . . It is, I suggest, a more lasting contribution than those made by the American and French Revolutions." The human subject, this "autonomous entity," this "human being who is more than the totality of his history," represents Jones's concession to what Tillyard calls the "timeless" values of tragedy, but he remained for Jones, in essence, the same being Sidney had defined as the hero of epic agency.[9] In *O Strange New World* Jones's epic "hero" shoulders the contradictions of Renaissance heritage and colonial hardship and rediscovers his classical heritage in a revolution that projects the homely virtues of republican Rome into an agrarian society. In *The Age of Energy,* this same epic hero embraces materialism, cosmopolitanism, and imperialism in a frenzied search for a sense of unity to replace the simpler federalist vision lost in the aftermath of the Civil War. Despite racism, pessimism, and withering provincial "monotony," American society maintains its heroic imperative. If Faustian man was Jones's idea of the epic-tragic hero of modern civilization, Theodore Roosevelt was his idea of the truly epic hero of turn-of-the-century America. In Roosevelt "Hamiltonian power" and "Jeffersonian democracy" were blended in a "practical idealism." Odysseus-Aeneas-Roosevelt embodied the destiny of his nation.

With a jaunty bitterness that recalls the 1965 postscript to his reissue of *The Theory of American Literature,* Jones attributed the demise of the "Age of Energy" to a combination of Freudianism, "denial," and "selling." "The test of public policy slowly shifted from Roosevelt's 'Is it

9. E. M. W. Tillyard, *The Epic Strain in the English Novel,* 15; HMJ, *Revolution and Romanticism,* 463–64.

righteous?' and Taft's 'Is it legal?' to the question: 'Will it be popular?' in opinion polls." In other words, the virtues of republican Rome had given way to the self-indulgence and luxury of the empire. The muses of epic—reason and ethics—had yielded their authority to urban realism, nonrepresentational forms, and various shades of popular approval. "Art was divorced not merely from tradition but from civism [*sic*] itself. The basis of rational dialogue between artist and spectator was eroded." Jones was particularly hard on the arts. Despite the ingenuity of the Armory Show of 1913, the upshot of the many innovations in painting, sculpture, and photography was that the arts had lost that great rush of energy that was still apparent in the sciences: "Never had the sciences been more brilliant—consider the list of American Nobel prize winners; never had technology done more . . . but in literature and the arts, as in advertising and 'selling,' the nonrational became king. The world of Thomas Jefferson was a lost world indeed." Jones's quarrel with the rejection of the "past" in the 1960s was foreshadowed in his disappointment over the failure of America's artists before World War I to see through the leveling dangers of the "international style." By uncritically joining Europe in cultural self-hatred, America was risking its own identity: "The long search for European values for which American sensibility might profit by associating itself with a great tradition here ended in a great denial of tradition."[10] One senses that Jones balks at the whiff of tragedy, that he wants America to stay its epic course.

The twists and turns of Jones's epic vision recall the episodic and fragmentary pacing of great English Romantic epics like *The Prelude, Don Juan,* and *The Idylls of the King.* His love of the nineteenth century, the seed time of his own soul, colored his historiography. Indeed, the Victorian coloring of Jones's Renaissance "picture" is not unlike the hue of Browning's Renaissance as the poet painted it in his famous dramatic monologues. Although he waited until the end of his life to give full credit to the Romanticism that had fired his own fiercely independent subjectivity, he was always the somewhat cynical and passionately curious Byronic narrator struggling to accommodate his Wordsworthian alterego, which would not allow him to diverge from the same social responsibility that informs Tennyson's poem. The scholar in Jones altered the terms of the Wordsworthian contract; instead of

10. HMJ, *Age of Energy,* 432–34.

the "Love of Nature leading to the Love of Man," for Jones, Love of Fact, with a gusto that recalls Browning's "barbarism" (Walter Bagehot's epithet for the poet), leads to the Love of Culture. Jones celebrates the phenomenological impulse in epic terms. Heroic facticity takes on all the power of *episteme.* When Frederic Jameson calls the contemporary range of "interpretive options" a "Homeric battlefield," he assigns to methodological variety the same heroic field that Jones found in phenomena themselves. Before things are named, they exist; or, to put it another way, once they are named, their existence is not preempted. "Metacommentary" was no problem for Jones. He did not interpret facts in a way that indebted him in any transcendent sense to other formulations of those facts. The facts themselves overflowed all conceivable commentaries, past or present, those of others or his own. Epic, as Aristotle pointed out, lacks the unity of tragedy. Indeed, epic has a contractual arrangement with experience; by not insisting on interpretative authority, it is permitted to view the entire range of Achilles' shield.[11]

Northrop Frye reminds us of the "encyclopaedic range" of "epic." Indeed, the synoptic presumption of epic inclusiveness risks self-indulgence in what can become a crippling device. The greatest temptation of the epic bard, whether Homeric, biblical, or Joycean, is to lean too heavily on cataloging the very phenomena that provide epic with its authority. The interminable lists of genealogy and military rank that almost demand excision in the Bible and Homer haunt Jones's voice and narration. He too loved his epic "lists" (dates, places, names) and would often extend them in his impressive orations as well as in his texts far beyond what even admirers thought necessary. He tended to forget Longinus's warning that excessive "amplification" loses its force "when not resting on a firm basis of the sublime." In his teaching this sometimes earned him the charge of pedantry. In his prose the effect can be that of an overloaded circuit, but often there is an ironic touch of intellectual self-mockery that reminds both writer and reader of the limitations of expository analysis. Induction and deduction are never entirely in adequate accord. Supportive evidence is either insufficient or excessive. Wolfgang Iser's phenomenological analysis of the reading of literary texts is based on the assumption that

11. James Korg, *Browning and Italy,* 62; Frederic Jameson, *The Prison-House of Language,* 13.

the writer's intention can in part control the reader's responses, but that the text always contains "gaps" or "indeterminate elements" that the reader must fill in through his subjective participation with the text. Jones would probably have agreed, but he would also have insisted that it is the writer's responsibility to educate as fully as possible the reader's contribution, not to stifle the reader's subjectivity but to prevent it from obliterating the writer's subject *and* object.[12]

We have already seen how thickly Jones could apply the trowel: ". . . the temperate landscapes of northern France, the Low Countries, the Germanies, and the British Isles." A series of Jones's, any series, had to be truly serial. "Pictures by Gerard Douw, de Hooch, Vermeer, and Maes lovingly insist upon tangible things in a bourgeois universe." Jones knew that most of his readers would recognize immediately the name of Vermeer van Delft and those who knew their art history might remember de Hooch. It is doubtful that the other two names would provide a spark, let alone the shock of recognition. Such a shock would require the reader's familiarity with the genre school of seventeenth-century Dutch painting. The point here is that the most famous name in the list, Vermeer, was a great master whose landscapes and portraits command as much attention as the intimacy of his interiors or the jewel quality of his fabrics. What he shared with the other painters in Jones's series, however, was primarily his skill as a painter of "tangible things"; Douw and Maes studied with Rembrandt and did portraiture, but they could not continue in the heroic tradition of their master's brooding and sublime humanism. De Hooch was the essential genre painter, known for the warmth of his domestic interiors. By simply adding Vermeer's name to the others, with no attempt to put it at the head of the class, Jones was stressing the growing materialism of the "Renaissance of the North," forcing the reader to confront the "gaps" in his knowledge. It is not sufficient, argued Jones, to know about Vermeer without knowing about his contemporaries—not if you want to know why he painted portraits *and* interiors and why he painted them both with equal passion. Admittedly, the idea of "gaps" in this context is different from Iser's notion of the creative participation of the reader with the text. Iser is talking about the reader of fiction or poetry. Jones wanted his reader

12. Northrop Frye, *Anatomy of Criticism: Four Essays,* 318; Longinus, "From the Sublime," in Bate, *Criticism: The Major Texts,* 66.

to be open to what history communicates, and this requires the reader to expand his models of understanding, to stretch to the utmost his willingness to absorb, retain, and digest information that on first glance may not seem pertinent. Jones wanted his reader to raise attentive capacities, to receive more of what was being communicated by the allusive range of the information he as a writer was sharing. The roster of warriors in *The Iliad* and the lists of ancestors in Genesis may seem to impede the flow of the action, but they continue to tease the anthropologist, philologist, historian, and hermeneuticist in us all.

For Jones the settling of Vermeer into that prosaic company captured the subtle attenuation of "character" in the Northern Renaissance into something closer to materialistic will. This line of thought was Jones's way of preparing for one of the boldest taxonomies in *O Strange New World.* Faced with the powerful materialism of colonial enterprise, Jones did not falter in his sense of the epic vision in American history. Sidney's high Renaissance notion of the moral power of the epic hero was qualified by Jones's Romantic irony, but epic remained the typological clue to America's historical sense of itself and therefore remained at the heart of Jones's historiography. "What crossed the Atlantic into the British mainland colonies was not, then, capitalism, but a theological sanction upon the credit-making virtues. These became so fully amalgamated with Christian values in the United States, they were taken as axiomatic, Christianity meant activism."[13]

Jones made no claims to having originated the connections between capitalism and religion in modern historiography. What he did not share with thinkers like Max Weber and R. H. Tawney was their insistence that these two institutions were fated to intertwine because of the nature of each. It was rather, Jones believed, the need to canonize self-sufficiency in the harsh and demanding environment of the colonies that forced early America to stretch moral sanctions provided by a religion grounded in charity and love to accommodate what often amounted to ruthless self-interest. However contradictory this essentially Protestant solution may seem in its European origin and context, where it takes on all the tragic misalignment Hegel's dialectical philosophy of history presumes to explain, in the context of the American experience it serves as a reasonable compromise and feeds the epic sweep of America's synthetic power.

13. HMJ, *O Strange New World,* 200.

After tracing the difficulties of reconciling "God and Mammon" from the very beginnings of civilization, Jones stressed the Protestant focus on "individualistic performance" as a substitute for the loss of "the confession as a mode of periodically relieving the soul of its sense of guilt." The devout Protestant faced the problem of reconciling his "performance in trade" with the demands of "Christian virtue":

> How was one simultaneously to gain riches and avoid the temptation inherent in them? By the doctrine of stewardship, which implied the stern self-discipline Protestantism imposed upon its followers. The qualities that made for success in commerce—sobriety, frugality, thrift, the credit-making virtues—were they not Christian virtues also? Business could be conducted with the high seriousness of religion; the self-sufficiency of the Protestant soul could be translated into the self-sufficiency of the moral tradesman. A thousand sermons, treatises, and essays adjured, warned, guided, and exhorted the Protestant middle class to get wealth, yet remain ascetic, grow rich but not relax their spiritual energy—Richard Baxter's *Saints Everlasting Rest* (1650), from which Weber draws, Richard Steele's *The Tradesman's Calling* (1684), which Tawney cites, Defoe's *The Compleat English Tradesman* (1725–1727), more worldly than either. Historians examine what Augustine, what Aquinas, what the medieval Jew, what Luther, what Calvin, what "painful Perkins," what a thousand others contribute to the doctrine that a businessman may be godly. Their investigations fascinate the reader, but it is here sufficient to remember that, however the doctrine of the gospel of wealth was put together, it became identified with the Protestant ethos, and that the New England colonies, New Amsterdam, Quaker Pennsylvania, the Swedes in Delaware, even Maryland (save for a brief period) were Protestant. Indeed, south of the Potomac, though there were worldly planters, there were more members of the middle class, and the Scotch-Irish in the Great Valley and in the Carolinas were as pawky Christians as was Baille Nicol Jarvie in *Rob Roy*. In American experience the ethos of Jonathan Edwards and the ethos of Benjamin Franklin are complementary, not opposed.[14]

What Jones accomplished in the above passage was to sharpen the difference between the European and American experience of the same dilemma. What required continuous apology in Europe (and Jones impishly integrates the famous and the obscure in his catalog)[15]

14. Ibid., 199.

15. Readers curious about the "medieval Jew" are sent in a footnote (*O Strange New World*, 422) to Clifford K. Shipton's "The Hebraic Background of Puritanism," but "painful Perkins" leaves the reader dangling. The index identifies him as William

was a social and geographic given in the predominately Protestant colonies. What seemed contradictory in the context of European religious and social history was in place almost from the beginning in America: "The ethos of Jonathan Edwards and the ethos of Benjamin Franklin are complementary, not opposed."

As I have noted earlier, Jones did not generalize easily. His skepticism took more readily to induction than deduction, and even when he found a resting place there was usually a tentative air. He was happiest when the range and intensity of his induction enabled him to expand or add to generalizations in place. The above example is typical. To separate Edwards and Franklin is to distort the continuity of American history; they are emanations of the same epic hero. Only a little more than a year before *O Strange New World*'s publication in 1964, Jones cited Van Wyck Brooks, who had recognized the "split" between "rationality" and "intuition" in the 1920s as evidence of a basic contradiction in American culture: "He [Brooks] said that one-half of America was descended from Benjamin Franklin the businessman and the other half from Jonathan Edwards the idealist." Jones's seeing of the connection between Franklin and Edwards as "complementary" rather than "opposed" transfigured Brooks's tragic dialectic, the Hegelian impasse of two positive forces, into an epic duality.[16]

Jones explored this duality-as-synthesis in great detail by carrying the idea from colonial theology through the revolutionary period and after: "By the end of the Napoleonic period interdenominational church groups, participating in the religious revivalism arising out of the reaction against the French Revolution and its aftermath, were establishing national societies that fused utilitarianism, patriotism, the encouragement of business enterprise, the Protestant ethic, and a theory that religion is a stabilizing force, into a single whole." Gradually, the "Protestant ethic" became attenuated and finally completely secularized. Under Theodore Roosevelt, for a historical moment, neither religion nor materialism was dominant: "The Franklinian emphasis upon the practical fuses with vigorous Christianity and social Darwinism."[17]

Perkins, but Jones knows that the average scholar-reader will be forced to the *DNB*. We are not permitted to assume that we know the theological background to the godliness of the businessman just because we may have read "Augustine . . . Aquinas . . . Luther . . . [and] Calvin."

16. HMJ, *Violence and Reason*, 56.

17. *O Strange New World*, 213, 220.

We have already noted how Jones's vision darkened when he finally had to concede that Faustian man, that ghost of European Romanticism, had more to do with modern consciousness, including American consciousness, than did Jefferson-Hamilton-Roosevelt. Struggling with this undeniably tragic realization, Jones Agonistes did not, in his old age, succumb to the postmodern temptation to see in a variety of determinisms (political, linguistic, anthropological) the solution to a liberation of older, more intractable determinisms, like religion and metaphysics. Just as he seemed to understand that "social Darwinism" could have its say without completely undermining pragmatic rationalism and strongly held religious convictions, Jones held on to the principle of subjectivity preserved in the dark heart of Faustian man as a guarantee of culture's ethical imperative. That imperative lay at the heart of epic. Jones did not desert the typology that had guided his study of culture from the earliest days. He did not forsake epic for the tropical vertigo of tragedy. Instead, he did what the epic bard is supposed to do. He picked up his lyre and retold the story. He went back to the beginning.

6

The Anacreontic Strain

Jones's interest in the transition from the Enlightenment to Romanticism lies at the center of his earliest studies in European intellectual history. It is also the subject of his last major work, *Revolution and Romanticism.* Just as the first work of the trilogy, *O Strange New World,* reclassified religious and ethical components (Edwards and Franklin) in order to highlight the epic integrity of the will to power in early American history, the last work reclassifies the philosophical, ethical, and psychological forces of the Enlightenment to effect a similar result. Jones wanted to clarify in the last work the subtle connections between rationalist and emotionalist ideas that fed the unifying surge of Romanticism. Unlike some postmodern thinkers who have gone to Romanticism in pursuit of its fragmentism and irrationalism to validate their fascination with indeterminacy, Jones cast a wider net to embrace contradictory forces that cultural historians have not always considered in concert, to illustrate the essential organicism of Faustian man, and to argue that his indestructible "subjectivity" confirms an ethical and metaphysical pact with an epic destiny that transcends the tragic anxiety of the modern world.

When he had Mephistopheles introduce Faust to the dubious pleasures of Auerbach's *Keller,* Goethe was giving ironic vent to the late eighteenth century's major formulation of the pleasure principle. Jones saw the trope of inebriation as ancillary to its typological home—what he called the "Anacreontic strain"—and he contrasted it to the idealism of the "Platonic strain" and the austerity of the "Plutarchian strain": "If the Platonic strain in neoclassicism furnished revolutionaries and romantics with ideal patterns in art, public life, philosophy and general life, the Plutarchian and stoic transition helped men to identify tyranny, to oppose it, and to will the means by which it was to be overthrown." To escape the moral demands of these two cultural norms, "the Anacreontic world," as Jones saw it, ignored politics, glorified the values of "youth, health, joy, love, and wine," and tried to forget time—"time that brings old age and death." Jones identified John Keats and Nicolas Poussin, Edna St. Vincent Millay and Dorothy Parker as representative of a "general Anacreontism" that has never disappeared since it first established itself in the sixth century B.C. "It is a human cry."[1] It is the distribution of these three conflicting typological strains in an organic formulation that speaks to the demands of "will" in the Romantic decades following the late Enlightenment and that informs Jones's grasp of a text like Melville's *Billy Budd*. As we saw in the comparison of Barbara Johnson and Jones on Melville's tale, her tropological difficulties with emplotment are somewhat obviated by Jones's direct assertions about will and character. His analysis is rooted in his understanding of the interplay between the three strains. Although Jones never applies them directly to *Billy Budd*, any reader must be struck by the illuminating relevance. Billy in his "youth, health, joy, and love" (only the labeling trope of "wine" is bracketed) is crushed between the agonized "Platonism" and irrefutable "Plutarchism" of Captain Vere. Billy's "God bless Captain Vere," his gallows speech at the tale's close, is the quintessential "human cry."

Jones's grasp of the importance of the Anacreontic strain as a connecting theme between Enlightenment and Romantic sensibility lay at the heart of his first major publication in Romantic studies, the same work that troubled the Harvard committee in 1936 when Conant urged the English department to consider him for a position. In *The Harp That Once*, Jones's book about Thomas Moore, the lyric poet and friend of Byron, he argued the centrality of Romantic Hellenism. Jones's knowledge of the whole Winckelman-Wackenroder-Schiller-Hölderlin-

1. HMJ, *Revolution and Romanticism*, 144–45.

Goethe heritage, which Heine ultimately ironized, made him unusually perceptive of the carryover of Greek motifs and ideas into the supposedly medievally oriented Romantic imagination. One must not, of course, ignore scholarship's awareness of the Hellenic strain in Romantic writers. Harry Levin, Jones's colleague at Harvard, had written a brilliant undergraduate essay on Romantic Hellenism, published as *The Broken Column* (1931), but by and large Byron, Shelley, Keats, and Poe were inaccurately seen as atypically Romantic in their fascination with Greek or classical themes. Jones's book, when it appeared in 1937 (the same year Douglas Bush's magisterial *Mythology and the Romantic Tradition in English Poetry* was published), helped to correct this misunderstanding by bracketing German literary Hellenism and stressing Hellenism in the architecture, landscape design, and the plastic and visual arts of late eighteenth-century England. It is precisely because Horace Walpole's Strawberry Hill was believed to have initiated Romantic medievalism in Britain that Jones challenged the semiotic authority of this eccentric pile by forcing it into an epic list that gives way to Hellenically inspired artists. In demonstrating a strong nonliterary Hellenism in this period, Jones establishes the cultural centrality of Greek sensibility at the time and thereby strengthens his case for the importance of Thomas Moore as a literary champion of a cultural humanism neglected by the majority of English Romantic writers in his day. The careful and detailed mounting of this historical argument makes a persuasive case for Moore as an important link between the traditional Hellenism of the Augustan Age and the important Hellenic poems of the second generation of Romantic poets:

> But more important than the showy learning is the impulse that the *Odes of Anacreon* helped to give to the literary revival of Hellenism which forms an important living element in the romantic movement. For the Augustan age antiquity had been Roman or, when it was Greek, Greek in the fashion of Johnson's *Irene.* Now antiquity was becoming warm, colorful, and Hellenistic. *The Antiquities of Athens* by Stuart and Revett, first published in 1762, began in 1787 a series of new editions. The Society of the Dilettanti brought back exciting reports of Greece under the rule of the Turks, and the Elgin Marbles were about to be transplanted from the blue sky of Hellas to the smoke of London. "Classical" architecture, which had begun by adopting Roman motives, ended by turning Greek, passing from austerity to gracility in the process, as Doric temples commenced to sprout on English lawns and the Greek fret or "anthemion" ran in long friezes over the heads of diners in

> the houses of noblemen. . . . The new mode had invaded painting to the disgust of Horace Walpole, who referred unclassically to Barry's Venus "standing stark naked in front and dragging herself up to Heaven by a pyramid of her own red hair"; but despite the petulance of the builder of Strawberry Hill, Barry, Fuseli, Flaxman, and others were to find flowing line and poetic coloring appropriate to the gods of Hellas. In literature the gap which separates Pope's Homer from Byron's *Childe Harold* had still to be bridged; Shelley's *Hellas* and Keats' *Lamia* must be prepared for; and there can be little doubt that the warmth, the eroticism, the lyricality of Moore's *Anacreon* led the way. Nor was its vogue transient; if one judges by the critical notices, laudatory verse, and biographical accounts evoked by the poet's growing celebrity, the translation continued to be extensively read three or four decades after it first appeared.[2]

Almost forty years after writing the above passage, Jones expanded his original insight into the bonding power of the Anacreontic strain. It was transformed from merely a link between eighteenth- and nineteenth-century taste in cultural matters into that "human cry" that, as noted above, he attributed to a "general Anacreontism" in place from the beginning of Western civilization. This was no trope for Jones, but rather a typologically powerful category for understanding social as well as cultural shifts in historical process. Jones's lifelong argument for the deep interrelatedness of European and American culture gained authority from the way he intertwined his archetype of Anacreontism with the other two typologies, Platonism and Plutarchism, to sketch a theory of cultural history that remained true to his epic vision without ignoring the tragic shadows. There was a psychological realism in Jones's sense of heroic man that encouraged him to distinguish "perfection" from "sublimity," to imagine human beings realizing their hopes for freedom without dashing themselves on the rocks of tragic overreaching:

> During and after any considerable war the expectation of death, the fear of dying, or a well-nigh hysterical obsession with the five senses as an affirmation of vitality is greater than in normal times. In such periods important elements in society find that patriotism and religion lose their appeal. A philosophy of "Eat, drink, and be merry, for tomorrow we may be shot" has an immediate allure to the young and to those who fear they are likely to be the next victims of the conqueror or the headsman. The Seven Years War developed an increase in luxury and gaiety all over the Western world. During the American revolution

2. HMJ, *The Harp That Once: A Chronicle of the Life of Thomas Moore*, 57–58.

> austerer patriots complained that in cities such as New York and Philadelphia (even Boston!) pleasure reigned when austerity should have prevailed. (One thinks of the Mischianza in Philadelphia in May 1778.) The hectic gaiety of imprisoned aristocrats during the French revolution, hourly expecting the tumbrel that would carry them to the guillotine, has passed into legend. Sensuality and corruption characterized Parisian life during the Terror and the Directorate. English society was never giddier than during the wars against the French Republic and Napoleon. . . .
>
> But there is another aspect to this relationship. The Anacreontic tradition, relaxed and anti-intellectual—youths passing the drinking bowl from hand to hand, maidens dancing in a fair meadow, shepherds and villagers who never pay taxes, the gods reduced to nymphs or satyrs, old men longing to be young, who put off the majesty of age in favor of Bacchic revelry—types such as these reduced classical man to human proportions. The Plutarchian hero was larger than life. Platonic idealism required thinking on an exalted level. But one could not live forever on the high plateau of Platonic idealism or imitate Cato's dyspeptic denunciation of the follies of mankind. The perfection of humanity is not necessarily sublimity. The idealized Greece (or Sicily) of Winckelman had to be peopled, but peopled by beings who were not demigods; and while it was admirable to elevate mankind, how high, so to speak, was the elevation to rise? Let us be nymphs and shepherds before we play the part of Prometheus.[3]

Jones's "nymphs and shepherds," on the surface a simple pastoral trope, are limned here to wear a distinctly human face. It is important to note the way Jones connected American revolutionary experience with his theory of Anacreontic release. He was clearly pleased that the birth of the United States was something of a synchronic embarrassment—indeed a fortunate diachronic accident. The new nation erupted shortly before Romanticism itself swept the Western world. What might have been a great celebration of Romantic excess—a new nation cutting itself off from the past and realized in the full bloom of its subjectivity—was instead a blueprint example of Enlightenment engineering. Reason remained in charge when the American rebels rejected George III. Platonic and Plutarchian strains were still very much in the air. As a result, the American consciousness has a more tempered notion of emotional release than the European, particularly when it comes to political behavior. Whereas Europeans embrace idiosyncrasy and cultivate individuality, Americans tend to the reason-

3. *Revolution and Romanticism*, 145–46.

able notion that everyone must have the liberty of his pleasures, but these must not necessarily be eccentric or mysteriously private. As Richard Chase observed in the 1950s, we are a conservative people with liberal institutions. In recent decades hippies have yielded to yuppies, and the new African American middle class is no more or less conservative than any middle class in our history.

Jones feared Freud's challenge to the tendency of repression in American cultural life. Too learned not to appreciate the tragic implications of this repression, Jones must have been aware that occasional violence in America of a peculiarly psychotic nature may very well be attributable to the repression resulting from what was originally thought a reasonable accommodation of the emotions. Nevertheless, for Jones excessive speculation about the subconscious courted the dangers of hubris and gambled away humanity for the dubious privileges of a semidivine Titanism. The "sublimity" of a Prometheus was not worth the birthright of one's human "perfection." One of Freud's greatest champions in contemporary literary theory has recently acknowledged certain contradictions in Freudian humanism that Jones's objections foreshadowed. It is particularly noteworthy that Harold Bloom begins the following paragraph in his *Ruin the Sacred Truths* with a salute to his former teacher, a scholar of Jones's generation who shared his reputation for wide and deep learning:

> My late teacher Frederick Pottle wrote an essay on Wordsworth and Freud called "The Theology of the Unconscious." I think that is the proper link; neither Wordsworth nor Freud was an unconscious theologian—yet both sought to replace a dying god with a new one, the god of the perpetually growing inner self. That makes them both descendants of my least favorite Biblical proclaimer, the unwholesome Jeremiah, but Wordsworth and Freud were much more benign than the hysterically powerful Jeremiah. Jeremiah had a positive passion for the destruction he lamented, while they had a profound affection for all of us and immense sympathy for our discomfort with culture. Nevertheless, I fear that Wordsworth and Freud were also responsible for writing the Law upon our inward parts, and thus completing the Enlightenment's program of internalizing all values. This seems an unjust indictment in the wake of Wordsworth's insistence upon the progressive and yet further humanization of the human heart by which we live, and of Freud's incessant emphasis upon reality testing. Otherness is the overt teaching of Wordsworth and of Freud, whether the other be the object of the heart's affections or the object of the drives. Yet there is something equivocal in the otherness, whether Freudian or Wordsworthian, be-

> cause tropologically such otherness itself is a kind of death, a figuration for one's own death.[4]

Just as Jones rejected the tropological glamour of Hamlet's fascination with the ultimate "Other" of his own death and dared to suggest that Claudius's earthly and human ambitions were made of healthier stuff, so he would have perked up at Bloom's comments, originally heard at Harvard in a Norton Lecture (had he lived long enough to attend it), and applauded his insights into the narcissism of modern sublimity. And yet Jones would have felt the irrepressible need to take issue with Bloom's way of wrenching "Otherness" free of its historical context in order to reassert the centrality of the egotistical sublime. It was *not* the "Enlightenment's program [to] internalize all values." *That* was Romanticism's doing. For all its contributions to the saving of subjectivity and individuality, a service to culture that we have already seen acknowledged by Jones, historical Romanticism was already beyond the nurture of the "Platonic, Plutarchian, Anacreontic" paradigm. Jones seemed to stop short of Hegel's idea of *Aufhebeung,* in which reason and emotion transcend their differences in a *Versöhnung,* or reconciliation, whereby reason can accept its imminence in *Geist.*[5] This suggests something close to metaphysical equivocation on Hegel's part and invites a slurring of the ethical imperative as Jones understood it. And this is precisely why Jones found himself as a cultural historian in the epic mode. What Hegel had dismissed as fixed in legends of the past, and therefore ethically suspect, became for Jones the cultural facts of the past and thus indicators of ethical possibility.

* * *

In his prescient essay of 1964, "Structuralism and Literary Criticism," Gérard Genette argued, "Noting the presence or absence, in isolation, of a literary form or theme at a particular point in diachronic evolution is meaningless until the synchronic study has shown the function of this element in the system. An element can remain while changing function, or on the contrary disappear while leaving its function to another." Genette, in other words, was persuaded that to pursue the codes of literature is to discover structures that transcend

4. *Ruin the Sacred Truths: Poetry and Belief from the Bible to the Present,* 131–32.
5. Charles Taylor, *Hegel and Modern Society,* 49.

local meaning. Jones spent a lifetime acquiring information; the patterns that these localized data assumed were finally the patterns made possible by an increasingly sophisticated grasp of the *story* of history, an epic narrative typologically secure enough to support the weight of diachronic plenitude without succumbing to the defining authority of a synchronic formula. Jones reversed Genette's priorities and trusted in diachronic complexity to generate its own deductive illumination. What Jones would *not* do was jump to the deconstructive conclusion that because facts outstrip any transcendent generalizations designed to discipline them, we must therefore fall back on and into tropological totalizing. "I can understand the theater of the absurd, but I do not care to remain, a helpless spectator, in its auditorium. I think men are often irrational, but I think man is rational." It is here that we can sharply distinguish Jones from the New Historicists. Their fascination with textual details invariably becomes an exploration of tropological import; statues, paintings, houses, marginal allusions of all sorts become small levers of incredible strength intended to lift the text toward a more illuminating light. For Jones details were mysteriously cumulative; they were dangerous in isolation but richly suggestive in their very confusion. Jones, however, did not permit himself the pleasures of an antiquarian lost in grottoes of glittering information. There were no resting places for the historical imagination, other than pinnacles towering over the caves and slopes of facticity.[6]

One such mountaintop was the paradigm Platonic-Plutarchian-Anacreontic. Jones reached it by meditating on the diachronic crossroad of the Enlightenment and Romanticism. The fact that the Anacreontic was a "human cry" and universal throughout history meant to Jones that it overshadows the particularities of its expression in the comic, tragic, or satiric modes. Its ontological authority prevents it from taking on the epistemological ambiguity to which the postmodern theorist is committed. In confusing ontology and epistemology, thinkers of every stripe are theorizing the phenomenal world in the image of its perceived functions rather than its reality.

I find revealing Genette's turning to Boris Tomachevski, the structuralist literary historian, for historical examples in support of his own theory of the "synchronic study" of "literary forms":

6. Gérard Genette, "Structuralism and Literary Criticism," 74; HMJ, *Violence and Reason*, 58–59.

> An element that has a particular value in a certain period will completely change its function in another period. The grotesque forms, which were regarded in the period of Classicism as resources for the comic, became, in the Romantic period, one of the sources of tragedy. It is in this continual change of function that the true life of the elements of the literary work are to be found.[7]

Tomachevski's examples in support of the changing function of the grotesque beg the historical question, whereas Jones's discoveries of the interplay between "hedonistic and heroic strains" provide texture to our understanding of Romantic Hellenism. What Tomachevski calls the "true life" of the literary work is a kind of wordplay in which interpretive ingenuity (the generic variety of the grotesque) is given ontological status. Jones's typologically grounded narrative history may very well enjoy revival as many readers become increasingly disenchanted with not only structuralist paradigms but also the poststructuralist rhetoric of indeterminacy that has succeeded them. At a symposium in the summer of 1989, Richard Rorty remarked:

> Theorists like Heidegger saw narrative as always a second-best, a propaedeutic to a grasp of something deeper than the visible detail, the true meaning behind the familiar and commonplace one. Novelists like Orwell and Dickens are inclined to see theory as always a second-best, never more than a reminder of a particular purpose, the purpose of telling a story better. I suggest that the history of social change in the modern West shows that the latter conception of the relation between narrative and theory is the more fruitful.

To tell the story of culture, Jones relied on the typologies suggested by the story itself. Historians influenced by the deconstructionist assumptions in Hayden White's historiography have attempted to break out of what they feel are the determinisms implicit in established narrative strategies by writing history as "collage." Data heretofore thought unconnected or discrete because they were locked in narrative structures that disguised or distorted their nature have been reassembled in new wholes, wholes that have no apparent logical or temporal connection. This, to repeat an earlier observation, is further illustration of postmodernism's insistence on confusing ontology and epistemology; shifting our linguistic and rhetorical perceptions does not diminish the intractability of reality.

7. "Structuralism and Literary Criticism," 75; the source is Boris Tomachevski, "La nouvelle école d'histoire littéraire en Russie," *Revue des etudes slaves* (1928): 238–39.

Although Jones himself could cast out far-flung nets to haul in obscure and marginal information, he would have rejected such a skeptical solution to the difficulties of presenting history through narrative. He could tolerate dissonance because he had an ear for hidden harmonies, the music of the historical spheres. Late in his life he wrote that the organization of his three great histories leaned on musical forms:

> The only word I can think of that will illuminate their structure is 'symphonic.' By this I mean that in each I seized upon three or four major themes and studied their development in American history as closely as I could. The trilogy is therefore not a consecutive history either of American culture or of American literature, but the intent of the whole was to analyze what was happening in the mainland colonies and the United States, not alone in the light of what seems important to us today but also in the light of our relations with the Old World.[8]

His "major themes" were the typologies that he drew from the epic range and purpose of what he considered the culture's story. He recognized the validity of stepping back from the diachronic imperative ("not a consecutive history"), and he knew about the "collective subjectivity" ("not . . . either American culture or American literature") that has energized postmodernism. In the end, however, he was convinced that tragic indeterminacy could not prevail, that the epic drummer would always have our ear:

> Present fashions in criticism and philosophy celebrate frustration and despair. But these, if life survives, will, like other fashions of the world, pass by, leaving the drama of heroism and compassion once more unobscured. The virtue of the present age, though we are loath to admit it, is compassion, but the meaning of charity, that greatest of the trinity in Paul's epistle, it is the intention of humane studies to enrich. The weakness of the present hour is its failure to sound the heroic note, but heroism is pictured in the humanities, heroism is infectious, and heroism needs to be rediscovered, whether it be found in the mystical death of an Oedipus at Colonnos or in the brassier but still inspiriting concept of Macaulay:
>
> And how can men die better
> Than facing fearful odds
> For the ashes of their fathers
> And the altars of their gods.

8. HMJ, *Autobiography,* 266.

No amount of statistical analysis will re-inforce love of country, no amount of psychiatric lore alter the truth of Juliet's love for young Romeo. Men are not moved by digital calculators, but by color and example. Moreover, if we are to retain civilization, we must lay hold upon those who have created the humanities. In encouraging right value judgments, humanism, without prejudice to the churches, still makes a central value judgment for all mankind, best phrased by William Blake when he wrote: "The worship of God is: Honoring his gifts in other men, each according to his genius, and loving the greatest men best."[9]

9. HMJ, *One Great Society*, 177–78.

7

The New Landscape

Jones's grounding in the typology of epic did not preclude a free and hearty indulgence in tropes. He enjoyed rhetorical play and would slip into archaisms and ironic reversals of tone with nothing less than gusto. For Jones tropes were resting places, not slippery edges. They focused; they did not dissipate. Perhaps the trope of which he was fondest was landscape.

This in no way suggests that he was tropologically centered after all. On the contrary, what attracted him to places, regions, and landscapes was the firmly held conviction that they embodied the epic possibilities of the American imagination: "In the nineteenth century the historian Francis Parkman, whose dozen volumes on the French and Indian wars are, some say, the prose epic of American literature, set himself the task of finding out what the experience of the wilderness in the eighteenth century had been." Jones went on in this section of *The Frontier in American Fiction* to quote from Parkman's descriptions of the Illinois territory and the teeming life of the prairies, the "countless bison" and the "loathsome beauty . . . of the moccasin." "In this superb passage," Jones concluded, "terror combines with fecundity as a characteristic of middle America." These midwestern opposites combined as readily as their eastern counterparts had in *O Strange New World:* "In American experience the ethos of Jonathan Edwards and the ethos of

Benjamin Franklin are complementary, not opposed." Readers will note that "terror" and "fecundity" in the American wilderness are not that different from the ethos of Edwards and the ethos of Franklin. Jones was in command of this irony, and it resonates throughout his work. It lies at the center of his faith in the epic diversity of America, in the nation's ability to overwhelm the divisive and potentially tragic pressures undermining unity with the possibilities implicit in its geographical plenitude. Just as the "Anacreontic strain" humanized the rational and moral demands of the "Platonic" and "Plutarchian" strains, landscape in American experience connects the sublime and the ordinary. In the following passage from the opening pages of what many felt was his best book, *The Age of Energy: Varieties of American Experience, 1865–1915,* Jones spelled out in great detail what he felt to be the principal cause of America's epic nature. We see here how the trope of geographical space confirms the typology of Jones's epic vision:

> But though the forces of change were powerful, the era never really attained either political or cultural unity. The United States remained essentially what it had been—a tumultuous republic, a nation under perpetual stress and strain. Despite the vast central area of prairies and plains, its terrain was, and is, extraordinarily diverse; a continental country that varies from alluvial deltas to the peaks of the Rockies and from sea-level swamps to the elevated deserts of Utah and New Mexico. Florida, or much of it, is subtropical; North Dakota shares the winters of central Canada. The lower Mississippi is one sort of river, the Colorado another, the Humboldt still a third. Lives in Alabama, in upper New York State, in Montana, and on the Eastern Shore of Maryland differed as greatly as life in the Mediterranean basin differed from life in Finland. The Old South had one feeling for history, Utah a second, Plymouth a third, and Santa Fe a fourth. If today the supermarket and the throughway, the motel and the filling station emphasize monotony, American feeling for time and distance is still tribal, local, and subjective: in the matter of patience compare a New York journalist, a wool-hat from Georgia, a New England lobsterman, a Negro in Savannah, and a Colorado forest ranger. This rich heterogeneity has latterly been increased by the admission of the forty-ninth and fiftieth states, since Alaska and Hawaii could scarcely differ more in location, climate, population, history, and economic outlook. But do they differ more in 1970 than Delaware differed from Minnesota in 1870?[1]

1. HMJ, *The Frontier in American Fiction: Four Lectures on the Relation of Landscape to Literature,* 16–17, 18; *O Strange New World,* 199–200; *Age of Energy,* 48–49.

Jones's "regionalism" may strike the contemporary reader as a dated form of classification, but we must remember that today's ethnic and feminist perspectives are just as heavily centered in urban worlds as older American sensibilities were centered in rural ones and that current American fiction is rediscovering barrio and ghetto. Robert Frost, who enjoyed Jones's friendship and support for many years (Jones was instrumental in getting Frost a temporary appointment to the English department at Harvard), shared Jones's passion for place. C. P. Snow records an interesting discussion he had with Frost on the matter:

> Then he spoke about what he called "the locative" in art. Art which meant anything to him was locative, rooted in a place, in the singularities of a place. We had a bit of an argument. Temperamentally, I said, I was on his side. But locative art needs knowledge and patience to understand: that was why cosmopolitan art, abstract art, travelled further and faster. One didn't have to *know* anything to read, say, Kafka or Hemingway. They had travelled round the world to an extent that Jane Austen or Forster never would. Frost wouldn't have it. The greatest locative art transcended everything. It was organic, and no other art could be. He still had immense stamina for argument, or rather for his oblique interpretation of ideas. He would have gone on talking long after our hosts returned.[2]

Frost's insistence on rooting the "organic" in the "locative" defines precisely Jones's strategy for securing the far-flung nets necessary to bring in historical synthesis. Historiography was finally a kind of landscape art in which the historian-painter trusted in the plenitude of phenomena connected with all those things and ideas emanating from a space that is contracted to time and nature. There is something Burkean in all this, a historicized empiricism. Contemporary thinkers will want to suggest Husserl. Jones would have opted for the Renaissance hierarchy discussed in Chapter 5: epic is the greatest genre because it provides the greatest ethical models; "historical landscapes" (and I am using landscape as a trope, not a type) enable us to entertain the possibility of ethical (heroic) action. There is no doubt that the "locative" threatens the modern *and* postmodern sensibility. Hegel's dismissal of the "epic-ethical" as a fantasy and his insistence on the "tragic" as the key to a modern idea of history was echoed by Charles Baudelaire in the "Salon of 1846": "As for historical landscape, over which I want to say a few words in the manner of a requiem mass, it is

2. *Variety of Men*, 198–99.

neither free fantasy, nor has it any connection with the admirable slavishness of the naturalists; it is ethics applied to nature. What a contradiction, and what a monstrosity! Nature has no other ethics but the brute facts, because Nature is her own ethics."[3]

Baudelaire was venting his spleen over a certain kind of academic painting, but his attitude foreshadows modern objectivity. Ten years after Baudelaire wrote the above, Matthew Arnold insisted that the object of criticism was to see the object as it actually was; however, he was holding out for the enlightened observer, the mind steeped in "sweetness and light" and sensitive enough to know that any objectivity that ignored the human need for "beauty and conduct" was simply not truly objective. Jones questioned Arnold's British elitism, but he identified with his idea of culture. Goethe's sensibility embodied the polarities of subjectivity and objectivity in a blend suitable for both Arnold and Jones. From the beginning to the end of his long life in art and thought, Goethe never wavered from his panoramic sense of the metaphysical connection between nature and ethics: "Nature's crown is love. Only through love can one approach her. . . . She is all. She rewards herself and punishes herself, pleases and tortures herself. . . . She is kind. I value her in all her works. She is cunning, but to a good purpose; it is best to ignore her cunning."[4]

If *Faust,* part 1, is a dramatic tragedy, *Faust,* part 2, is a dramatic epic. The greatest drama of the nineteenth century moves in a direction different from what Hegel felt would be the destiny of modern art and history. Faust, like Odysseus, wanders in worlds natural and supernatural and is finally "saved" after draining a swamp—saving a landscape. Jones's epic history, his "historical landscape" of America, his trust in the "locative" and "organic" all merge in what I would like to call an iconic pictorialism. Jones's historiography takes on the march of a frieze. Each page is a metope in which ideas and artifacts, men and events stand out against culture and region, time and space, like sculptures in a bas-relief. These are not individual sculptures we can see in the round; if we could, we would see less. This is precisely the paradox underlying all of Jones's teaching and writing. It is the very thing that made his critics accuse him of confusing background and foreground.

3. *The Mirror of Art: Critical Studies,* 112.

4. From Johann Wolfgang von Goethe's early prose poem "Die Natur" (1782), in *Werke in Zwei Bänden,* 2:961–62 (my translation).

We have already seen one of Jones's landscapes—the "maps" of the northern and southern Renaissance. Although Ruskin and Pater are the precursors here, Jones probably became persuaded of the rhetorical power of thinking in landscapes from what he had discovered in Parkman and the American novelists of the nineteenth century—particularly Cooper. In his essay "Prose and Pictures: James Fenimore Cooper," originally given as an address at the 1951 Cooper Centennial in Cooperstown, New York, Jones traces Cooper's close connection with prominent painters of the Hudson River school and documents both Cooper's reliance on the painters for his passages describing landscape and the painters' reliance on his novels for their choice of subjects for their canvases. "The relationship of landscape painting by the Hudson River school to Cooper's fictional technique and to his view of life is matter of considerable import," argues Jones. He continues with the following observation:

> In *Precaution* landscape is not a problem, for the natural setting does not exist; but in novels like *The Pioneers, The Pilot, The Last of the Mohicans,* and *The Prairie* landscape is central to the book. Now the characteristic formula for landscapes by the founders of the Hudson River school is this: a dark foreground, usually with one or two trees, commonly dead, and tiny figures looking into the picture; theatrical perspective, so that one views as from a height a vast expanse; winding water in the middle distance extending to the plain of the horizon; the highlight of the central scene and on the distant sky; and silvery cloud or vapor shedding sentiment and vagueness over interminable leagues of earth beyond. This combination of the picturesque and the sublime is evident in most of Cole's landscapes, in works like Doughty's *The Raft* and in Asher B. Durand's *Kindred Spirits,* where Thomas Cole and William Cullen Bryant are portrayed admiring a mountain waterfall (they look *into* the picture), and the tree, not blasted this time, occupies a fourth of the canvas.[5]

The "tiny figures" and the "vast expanse," "picturesque" and "sublime," the foreground and the background: all this recalls the binary structures we have seen throughout Jones's own work. Despite poststructuralism's doctrine on binary structure, namely, that it inevitably deconstructs whatever it embodies—the world as oxymoron—there is an enabling connection between the point of view of the insignifi-

5. "Prose and Pictures: James Fenimore Cooper," in *History and the Contemporary,* 68–70; first published in *Tulane Studies in English* 3 (1952): 133–54.

cant figure and the overwhelming grandeur of the observed landscape. It is as if the sublimity of the expanse were dependent on the vulnerable charm of the picturesque observer. Only the mind that cannot know it all can know it at all. This is not nescience. As in our discussion of Jones on Poe, the "tiny reader" (Jones as historical critic) can step back far enough to see the text in history and not just history in the text. The former approach is the way of traditional cultural history; the latter is akin to what in recent years we have come to call New Historicism, which narrows "history" to what we can discover in and between the lines, not to mention the margins, of the text. "A major strength of the movement [New Historicism]," according to Don E. Wayne, "lies in the way it has acknowledged and elucidated the textuality of history and the intertextual relations between canonical literary texts and other kinds of cultural data."[6] There is a touch of the old positivism in the "new" historicism; knowledge becomes harder, more concrete—what the Germans call *sachlich*—but the resulting *episteme* brackets history itself while the text steps forward in historical monism. Jones welcomed intertextuality between "canonical texts" and "cultural data" long before the term *New Historicism* was coined, but he did not believe that texts reified history; on the contrary, the more texts, any texts, were read, the more they seemed to dissolve into something transtextual, or history itself. To achieve unity in his writing, Jones had to literally create landscapes large enough to enclose the range of suggestibility inherent in texts and in data.

Blake Nevius acknowledges Jones's pioneering of our understanding of Cooper's connection to the Hudson River school and theorizes a structure in Cooper's fiction that is similar to what I am asserting here about Jones's historiography. "The unity of the composition [of Cooper's descriptive landscapes] is achieved not through a governing schema, but eventually through a perspective."[7] Jones illustrates Cooper's perspectivism by presenting a long passage from *The Last of the Mohicans:*

> Keeping this formula in mind, let us see how Cooper manages to render Lake George, the setting for the tragic events of *The Last of the Mohicans.* Hawkeye and his companions, Duncan Heyward, the two girls, and the two Mohicans, have escaped from their foes long enough

6. "The New Historicism."
7. Blake Nevius, *Cooper's Landscapes: An Essay on the Picturesque Vision,* 110.

to climb a mountain overhanging the lake, and now look on the landscape under the morning sun, their own backs being turned to the light. Here is how Cooper marshals his words:

> The mountain on which they stood, elevated, perhaps, a thousand feet in the air, was a high cone that rose a little in advance of that range which stretches for miles along the western shores of the lake, until meeting its sister piles, beyond the water, it ran off toward the Canadas, in confused and broken masses of rock thinly sprinkled with evergreens. Immediately at the feet of the party, the southern shore of the Horicon [Lake George] swept in a broad semicircle from mountain to mountain, marking a wild strand, that soon rose into an uneven and somewhat elevated plain. To the north, stretched the limpid, and, as it appeared from that dizzy height, the narrow sheet of the 'holy lake,' indented with numberless bays, embellished by fantastic headlands, and dotted with countless islands. At the distance of a few leagues, the bed of the waters became lost among mountains, or was wrapped in the masses of vapor that came slowly rolling along their bosom, before a light morning air. But a narrow opening between the crests of the hills pointed out the passage by which they found their way still further north, to spread their pure and ample sheets again, before pouring out their tribute into the distant Champlain. To the south stretched the defile, or rather broken plain. . . . For several miles in this direction, the mountains appeared reluctant to yield their dominion, but within reach of the eye they diverged, and finally united into the level and sandy lands, across which we have accompanied our adventurers. . . . Along both ranges of hills, which bounded the opposite sides of the lake and valley, clouds of light vapor were rising in spiral wreaths from the uninhabited woods, looking like the smokes of hidden cottages; or rolled lazily down the declivities, to mingle with the fogs of the lower land. A singular, solitary, snow-white cloud floated above the valley, and marked the spot beneath which lay the silent pool. . . .

I shall not quote the rest of the description, but at the feet of the observers lie the "extensive earthen ramparts and low buildings" of Fort William Henry, seen in specific detail. Is not this uncommonly like a description of a Hudson River school canvas? It is all there except the tree.[8]

In his own histories Jones cast himself as the "tiny" but puckish writer who could walk through historical landscapes large enough to yield

8. *History and the Contemporary*, 70–71 (the passages from Cooper's novels are from the Household edition of the *Works*, 32 vols., as reprinted by P. F. Collier and Son, New York).

intellectual discoveries analogous to the "singular, solitary, snow white cloud" that "floated above the valley and marked the spot beneath which lay the silent pool." The discovery of the "cloud" and the "pool" it reveals—an epic quest—comes only after the eye has scanned the entire horizon and composed a perspective that makes it possible to distinguish carefully what mountain, land, and sky have to offer in every direction of the compass.

Patiently, pugnaciously (in ironic counterpoint to the heroic expectations of the epic historian), and always aware of the "picturesque" position of the historian vis-à-vis the "sublimity" of his subject, Jones mapped his landscapes with the analytical skill of a cartographer who cannot forget that maps flatten and distort, that they are never the final word on what they depict. "You revise all the previous maps," exclaimed his former student and lifelong friend Walter Rideout after reading *The Age of Energy*. Justin Kaplan, referring to the same text, called it, perhaps more appropriately than he realized, "the landscape of half a century."[9]

By taking on a space so vast—the horizon as subject—Jones astonished with whatever order he discovered. Many of his readers have found him breathless for the effort. Others have marveled at his stamina, at his perceptual powers. Wallace Stegner used a trope of his own to capture Jones's revelatory powers, but that trope gives way to Stegner's generous humor, his need to find words and images that would do justice to the intellectual reach of what Jones had written:

> I have read the Age of Energy, and turned off the engines in order to think, but away off in the corners, among the twisty cams and gears, little wheels are still turning, and little eccentrics moving, and little reciprocating parts shuttling away. It is a book which, however trodden on, will twitch till sundown, and maybe beyond—and never mind how a Rube Goldberg machine became a serpent. You, knowing as much as you do, will have to answer to that one too. You know too damned much. You are a despair in my bowels. Doesn't *anything* ever leak away and get lost? Have you done nothing but read and think for seventy years? As Mr. Whatsisname said to Senator McCarthy, have you no shame? You make it very hard for the rest of us, who do forget things, who haven't read everything, who don't see connections automatically. I, to cite you a meager example, read and labor for three or four or five

9. Walter Rideout to HMJ, August 5, 1972, Walter Rideout's personal papers; and Justin Kaplan to HMJ, April 14, 1972, Jones Papers, Harvard University Archives, Cambridge.

years getting together a little historical machine made up of string and a few spools, and write it up and issue it with a sense of fatuous satisfaction, and then it has to be set up in the same World's Columbian Exposition with that Dynamo-Virgin-Behemoth-Leviathan-Atom-Smasher thing of yours. For the sake of us meager historians I hope the reading public is as unable to read as my experience tells me it is: for your sake, I hope it for once extends and exerts itself to come up to the dignity and magnitude of your book. As I read—and I read every word with my finger—I kept thinking of all the Mark Sullivans and Oberholtzers and Nevinses and Kazins and Ziffs it would take to match what was in my hands, between one set of paper covers, and I came out with a respect that is near-about-awe. You have enlarged me, Sir, but you broke some uncomfortable adhesions in the process.[10]

Denis Donoghue noted that in the first chapter of his *Lion and the Honeycomb,* R. P. Blackmur said that Henry Adams "used to argue that the great question was whether the American mind could catch up with American energy: he doubted it, but thought a good jump might do it." Jones's muscular intellectualism, particularly in *The Age of Energy,* was directed toward nothing less than making the "jump." In a period of American history when "energy" was at its peak, the cultural historian committed to interpretation was forced into a jump equivalent to a philosophical leap. Donoghue focused on Blackmur's sensitivity to Adams's "poetics of ignorance," an idea Adams crystallized in the observation that "true ignorance approaches the infinite more nearly than any amount of knowledge can do." Donoghue was finally impressed by a "glowing sentence" in which Blackmur captured the essence of what Adams meant: "One has to possess one's ignorance like knowledge." Donoghue elucidated: "The nineteenth century, according to Adams, was indifferent to what it could not understand: it did not possess true ignorance." Blackmur came to believe in a kind of authentic symbolization (symbols that "held in reserve the power of the occult, the mysterious, the unknowable") as insurance against the loss of "true ignorance"; this protective strategy became the way of American formalism.[11] For Derrida and the postmoderns "true ignorance" is preserved in "indeterminacy."

Jones certainly respected symbols (Faustian man, Roman architecture and the American republic, et cetera), but at the same time his

10. Wallace Stegner to HMJ, June 28, 1971, Wallace Stegner's personal papers.
11. Donoghue, foreword to *Henry Adams,* by R. P. Blackmur, ix, xiii.

passion for lists and "catalogues" rivals the deconstructionist's chase after traces. And he would have agreed with Donoghue's assessment of the nineteenth century's excessive materialism, but—and this is of vital importance—he would not have dismissed the nineteenth century's relation to "true ignorance" as "indifferent." On the contrary, "the great century was in truth overwhelmed and embarrassed by the revelation of its cultural inheritances—the cult of the North (as in Wagner's music dramas), the cult of the Slav (as in the vogue of Russian fiction), the cult of the Indian (as in Latin-American poetry and the twentieth-century Dartmouth College Library murals)." Jones saw the nineteenth century as drowning in a plenitude of history, scientific discovery, and political and cultural upheaval. In a very real sense "true ignorance" was less a matter of metaphysical awareness than it was simply not knowing enough of what could be known in the world of experience. Certainly Jones was not indifferent to religion or the "mysterious and unknowable," as his own cultural studies and professional service make clear. In the late 1950s he had chaired the Weil Institute, "an endowment intended to strengthen the bonds between theology and the humanities"; in 1967 he published *Belief and Disbelief in American Literature.* What the nineteenth century could not understand, to revise Donoghue's judgment, was the notion that "true ignorance" was somehow the achievement of a disinterested contemplation rather than the inevitable result of all thoughts and actions involving human beings. Except for their insistence on downplaying the subjectivity of the human individual, there is more of an understanding between Jones's empirical historicism and the collective subjectivity of the postmoderns than would seem to be the case. "The age of Goethe and Darwin, of Liebig and Thomas Edison could not separate human affairs from the contemplation of cosmic harmonies. Human affairs were part of the cosmos, part of the hurry and bustle, the conflict and collision of the universe."[12] Of course, for Jones this connection humanized the cosmos; it did not technologize man as in Heidegger and Foucault. The "human cry" rose above the din of the universe.

This, then, explains once again Jones's passion for erudition, for

12. HMJ, "The Greatness of the Nineteenth Century," in *History and the Contemporary,* 29, 36; previously published in *Harvard Library Bulletin* 11 (Winter 1957): 5–20. *Autobiography,* 245–46.

getting at as many of the facts as often as possible. There was no "true ignorance" without facts. One had, indeed, as Blackmur had said of Henry Adams, "to possess one's ignorance like knowledge." Despite the hermeneutic thrust of post-Nietzschean discourse, in which interpretation is its own knowledge, Jones never acceded to modern wisdom on what constituted true knowledge. He held out for the facts. He did not learn to sneer at erudition by dismissing it as pedantry. He knew enough to know that what he knew did not condemn him to antiquarianism. The more responsibility he assumed for the facts, the closer he remained to that "true ignorance" that protected him from premature theorizing. The demands of erudition prevented the scholar from lapsing into intellectual narcissism, from confusing the resting places of his thought, whether typological *or* tropological, with teleological discoveries. Jones never permitted himself to forget that there was a landscape out there and that he must not confuse the tree at his elbow with the forest spreading before him.

* * *

Jones began *O Strange New World* with a review of Europe's difficulty in picturing, mapping, *seeing* the landscapes it had discovered in the fifteenth and sixteenth centuries. By the time he wrote of the United States' birth at the end of the eighteenth century, the problem of simply recording a new world's appearance had gradually turned into a problem of historical self-discovery, what I have already described as an epic quest. The complex strains of Renaissance, colonial, and classical heritage feeding the identity of the new nation constituted the heart of Jones's book. As he came to closure, he returned to the question of landscape, now very emphatically a trope rather than a literal subject. Ostensibly a discussion about American landscape painting in the nineteenth century, Jones's last chapter, "American Landscape," returned to the same ideas and passages (Cooper and Parkman) that he had introduced some fifteen and ten years earlier. His new purpose was to subordinate the panoramic canvas of the Hudson River school to the imagination of Thomas Jefferson, his greatest epic hero. Jones included a long excerpt from Jefferson's *Notes on Virginia*, in which Jefferson created the "full panoramic landscape":

> The full panoramic landscape organized in aesthetic principles was, however, the special creation of Thomas Jefferson in his *Notes on Vir-*

ginia. In this book he did it twice: once in describing the Natural Bridge, and once in describing the confluence of the Shenandoah and the Potomac. Let us look at one of these famous set pieces:

> The passage of the Potomac through the Blue Ridge is, perhaps, one of the most stupendous scenes in nature. You stand on a very high point of land. On your right comes up the Shendandoah, having ranged along the foot of the mountain an hundred miles to seek a vent. On your left approaches the Potomac, in quest of a passage also. In the moment of their junction, they rush together against the mountain, rend it asunder, and pass off to the sea. The first glance of this scene hurries our senses into the opinion, that this earth has been created in time, that the mountains were formed first, that the rivers began to flow afterwards, that in this place, particularly, they have been dammed up by the Blue Ridge of mountains, and have formed an ocean which filled the whole valley; that continuing to rise they have at length broken over at this spot, and have torn the mountain down from its summit to its base. The piles of rock on each hand, particularly on the Shenandoah, the evident marks of their disrupture and avulsion from their beds by the most powerful agents of nature, corroborate the impression. But the distant finishing which nature has given to the picture, is of a very different character. It is a true contrast to the foreground. It is as placid and delightful as that is wild and tremendous. For the mountain being cloven asunder, she presents to your eye, through the cleft, a small catch of smooth blue horizon, at an infinite distance in the plain country, inviting you, as it were, from the riot and tumult roaring around, to pass through the breach and participate of the calm below. Here the eye ultimately composes itself; and that way, too, the road happens actually to lead. You cross the Potomac above the junction, pass along its side through the base of the mountain for three miles, its terrible precipices hanging in fragments over you, and within about twenty miles reach Fredericktown, and the fine country round that. This scene is worth a voyage across the Atlantic.

I quote this description in extenso because of the important elements of which it is composed. It is in the first place both panoramic and painterly, and its general pattern is that of a good many landscapes of the future Hudson River School. In the second place Jefferson insists upon vastness and upon the allure of the distant, that "small catch of smooth blue horizon" which invites one to pass through the breach of the mountains, though "at an infinite distance in the plain country," and find eventual peace. In the third place the vastness of space leads him to meditate upon vastness in time: his imagination goes back to the beginning of the New World when the Blue Ridge dammed up an ocean. Finally there are artfully inwoven suggestions of gigantic force that has

> left awe-inspiring evidence behind—the mountains have been rent asunder, the rivers have torn them from summit to base, in this wild and tremendous scene the rocks are evidence of "disrupture and avulsion," the waters (and the winds?) give forth riot and tumult "roaring around," and terrible precipices hang over one in fragments as one seeks the "fine country" beyond the wilderness. The accuracy of Jefferson's geology is not here in question, but only the cunning of his pen and his sense of the vast and powerful in landscape, the melodramatic history of the empty New World over endless stretches of time.[13]

Jefferson's Hellenic idealism and his passion for *Paidea,* the idea that a culture achieves perfection through education, provide the incentive for democracy to create the greatest opportunity for the spread of beauty and truth. This expansive vision of human perfectibility in time was captured, Jones believed, in the heroic spaces of the Hudson River school and its disciples. Jones knew that he had no binding evidence for the influence of Jefferson's nature writing in *Notes on Virginia* ("the Jefferson principle of panorama") on the Hudson school of painters, but by this time he knew that he himself had become a panoramic historian and that his commitment to the "perspectivism" that informs Cooper's narrative position (as the tiny figure in the foreground) must speak for his deepest convictions as historian and writer. Jones trusted the visionary guidance of the polymathic genius. Where Jefferson and Goethe led, he, the mere historian, might follow:

> How was pygmy man not merely to subdue the wilderness but also found an enduring republic? Landscape could teach him that he might be, and frequently was, at the mercy of great natural forces, yet if he would but penetrate into the beauty and harmony of the whole, if he would set himself to understand the dynamism of the world, all, under God, might go well. The doctrine was curiously parallel to that of Goethe's *Faust.*[14]

It is not difficult to imagine what a deconstructionist would do with the following passage, which comes from the paragraph immediately following the one quoted from above:

> Domestic landscapes painted by the Hudson River school (and its allies) commonly show diminutive figures in the foreground working at outdoor tasks, departing for church, fishing, or, as in Durand's "Mohawk Valley," contemplating nature. But beyond the farm, or the vil-

13. *O Strange New World,* 358–59.
14. Ibid., 362.

> lage, or the church, or the meadow, or the fishing pool, or the picnic spot, or the park, there lies vast extended nature—shimmering skies, a mysterious mist, mountains that block the view, vistas that compel the eye to climb upward through the picture and lose itself in a vague and immense distance.

Jones's answer to any suggestion that his "eye" losing "itself in a vague and immense distance" precluded any possibility of penetrating "into the beauty and harmony of the whole" would simply be that there was no contradiction whatsoever. Without the immense distance there was no possibility of encountering the plenitude necessary for a truly integrated vision.[15] One might also remind deconstructionists that their revelations of contradiction are no less dependent on the cosmic range of their canvases. Their landscape is language; Jones's was nature. Jones would laugh at the notion that nature was a creation of language. He would kick the proverbial stone.

It was Jefferson's vast intellect that resonated in his grasp of the literal expanse of American spaces. Jones sees this tendency to look to American horizons for symbolic confirmation of America's political idealism as endemic to American thought. When the "Christian geologist" Edward Hitchcock stood at the top of Mount Washington at midcentury, "there seemed to him to exist a working connection between the grandeur of God on Mount Washington and the theory of republican society." In "The Prairies," a book of poems published in 1832, William Cullen Bryant fused "personal observations, conjectures about the Mound Builders, and a theory of history. If the prairie gave his eye an endless field of sight, brooding on the past gave his imagination an endless field in time."[16] This epic field reminds us of Wordsworth's discovery in Book VI of *The Prelude* (1805) when, years after his descent from Alpine heights, he is possessed by the idea of the creative imagination; his "idea" of the mountain peak eventually far exceeds in grandeur the physical experience of standing there.

O Strange New World ends with "American Landscape." *The Age of Energy* begins with "American Panorama." The two chapters form a watershed with Jones standing at the top of the pass very much like Jefferson when he exercised his "principle of panorama" describing

15. Barbara Novak, "On Divers Themes from Nature: A Selection of Texts," 59–106.

16. HMJ, *O Strange New World*, 366, 367. See also his "Landscape as Religion: Irving, Bryant, Cooper," in *Belief and Disbelief in American Literature*, 24–47.

the confluence of the Shenandoah and the Potomac. What Jones sees as he surveys the transition from the earlier to the later part of the nineteenth century in America is a profound broadening and deepening of the landscape of space into the landscape of thought in time, a thought that must rise in imagination to deal with the endless contradictions swirling in the air. Materialism and idealism, science and theology, privilege and elitism—all seem to contend for primacy and all lay claim to the principle of vitalism. "If one looks more closely into this fascinating age, another general formula appears amid the eclecticism and the contradictions: the search for some sort of unifying law or principle in every important field of endeavor."[17]

Wallace Stegner knew his man when he flattered Jones by comparing *The Age of Energy* to an exhibit at the "World's Columbian Exposition"—"that Dynamo-Virgin-Behemoth-Leviathan-Atom-Smasher thing of yours." The ghost of Henry Adams hovers quite clearly over this compliment, and one cannot help feeling that Stegner's irony points to the problematic affinity between Jones and Adams discussed earlier in this chapter. Certainly Jones shared with his great precursor a visionary response to the World Columbian Exposition of 1893. For Jones the "Exposition" was a Wordsworthian "spot in time," a landscape of architecture, statuary, and light that conveyed the essence of America's capacity for wonder at the turn of the century. Adams, on the other hand, was put off by "the lowest fakes of the Midway" but conceded that "surely the Fair is a seductive vanity." After the contempt of the following—"Since Noah's Ark, no such Babel of loose and ill-jointed, such vague and ill-defined and unrelated thoughts and half-thoughts and experimental outcries as the Exposition, had ever ruffled the Lakes"—Adams risked contradiction with this oracular observation: "Chicago was the first expression of American thought as a unity; one must start there."[18] Blackmur, in his book on Henry Adams, the culmination of a lifelong interest but not published until 1980, some fifteen years after Blackmur's death, explains the paradox of Adams's reaction to the Exposition of 1893 in this manner:

> The Exposition at Chicago, to which Adams addressed himself . . . showed both a unity and a break in sequence: it seemed a natural product of the Northwest, but in achieving its character it had skipped

17. *Age of Energy*, 19.
18. *The Letters of Henry Adams, 1892–1918*, 33.

> London and New York. The art was trader's classicism with a look of unity. Therefore, Adams sat under Richard Hunt's dome as on the steps of Ara Coeli. History persisted in asking freshly the old question about the breaches in its own sequence. Showing the materials in motion, and showing art in arbitrary assertion of inexplicable meaning, "Chicago asked in 1893 for the first time the question whether the American people knew where they were driving." The art of the Exposition and the more astonishing fact of its existence were inexplicable, but the industrial exhibits at least suggested a kind of frame for more precise questions, because there it was possible to move from the known to the unknown.[19]

Jones knew Blackmur's essays on Adams, which dated back to 1936, but he would not have been familiar with the posthumously published work of 1980, the year of his own death. Certainly, Jones would have taken issue with the notion that the art of the exposition was "inexplicable" whereas the "industrial exhibits" provided the true clues to an emerging "unity." Jones was deeply skeptical of any attempt to oversimplify the variety of contradictory elements in the years 1865–1915, the years that he had defined as "The Age of Energy" in the title of his book and had signified even more sharply with the subtitle: "Varieties of American Experience." The pun on William James's famous title was egregiously intentional. In the preface to this work Jones acknowledged Henry Adams as the principal painter of the historical landscape embracing this dynamic period. In his famous intellectual autobiography, Adams had done his self-portrait with the age as background. He did not, however, Jones felt, get it quite right:

> All great periods have their characteristic motions of tension and release. What is the conflict at the heart of these fifty years? I think it is hinted at in the concluding chapters of *The Education of Henry Adams:* we have to deal with a tension between unity and multiplicity. Yet to set this forth as a bare central doctrine does not really shed light. Adams confined himself to the effects of science, invention, and industry upon the creation and control of physical (mechanical) energy. My guess is that the conflict was more complicated.
>
> In truth the tension between unity and multiplicity could not be reduced to the simplicity of a battle between the Virgin and the Dynamo. On the one hand, after Appomattox the drive for general order, for restoration, for a national policy, an American philosophy, an American idiom in the arts, in literature, in theology, in other forms of thought. On the other hand, the inexpugnable desire of major regions

19. *Henry Adams,* 104.

> in a continental empire to remain themselves, the belief that American culture was not created for uniformity but for variety (hence the local-color schools), the concept that if the federal government now over-arched the states, regionalism and the richness of imported alien cultures might be simultaneously fused into a useful outlook and yet retain their autonomy, their quality, and their color. After the Civil War the nation for the most part threw off its fear of Europe. It felt that Japanese, Chinese, Hindu, Turkish, Egyptian, and even Amerindian patterns of art and thought had something to contribute to a representative republic. After 1865 the wounds of war healed so slowly that even in 1970 they are still raw; yet a united nation pushed out to take in Alaska, Hawaii, Cuba, Puerto Rico, Guam, the Philippines, and various other parcels of real estate, including the Panama Canal Zone. The opposition to these measures, at best weak, was seldom sectional. The same decades that developed toward a restatement of one-hundred-per-cent Americanism saw opera, the museum, the university, the magazine, architecture and the book trade bringing to Columbia, the gem of the ocean, treasures and traditions from the total globe. At the same time, American specialists studied the archaeology of Yucatan or ancient Egypt, American historians wrote about Italy and the Inquisition, American scholars staffed the classical school in Rome, American businessmen furnished oil for the lamps of China.[20]

The way Jones interweaves reflections on national aspirations with observations on the persistence of regional and parochial values in the above passage speaks for his readiness, always, to embrace the contradictions of high and low, elitist and popular, in order to get closer to the truth of America without ignoring any games or players. This thrust in his thinking is motivated by his scholarly conscience and his innate liberalism. Fidelity to the evidence of the past blends with a tolerance of the demands of the present in such a way as to feed the sense of epic possibility. It was Adams's tragic either/or, his Hegelian absolutism of opposites—Virgin and Dynamo—that made Jones nervous. The current debate between multiculturalists and traditionalists is becoming more rancorous precisely because each party is denying the other any room to maneuver. Thirty years ago Leo Marx remarked on the American appetite for "doubleness": "The apocalyptic image of the Dynamo and the Virgin is the ultimate expression of the tragic doubleness that Adams locates at the center of modern history. To be sure the encounter with the machine is a portentous event in earlier works of the American

20. HMJ, *Age of Energy,* xiii–xiv.

imagination. In *Walden* and *Moby Dick* and *Huckleberry Finn* it creates awe and terror and a sense of powerlessness."[21]

Postmodernism, as I have already suggested, has helped maintain "tragic" polarization by leaning too heavily on deconstructionist perceptions of the past as suffering from *epistemes* stillborn because they were conceived in language unaware of itself. Jones stands as a corrective to the continuing tendency to settle for tragically binary myths. For Jones the culture of the past could no more be pushed aside than the politics of the present. What fascinated him in late nineteenth-century American history was the way in which both variety and unity, the temporary and the traditional, were being pursued with an energy that precluded their separation or any kind of hierarchical judgment. This insight represented a dramatic change in his own thinking from the binary structures of *O Strange New World*. The actor-director in him had deferred to the landscape painter. The switch from one trope to the other served the epic typology of his historiography.

* * *

Jones knew that, economically and socially, industry and technology by the end of the nineteenth century had more or less brought under control the conflicting forces of idealism and materialism in American life. Carnegie's philanthropy, particularly his endowment of free public libraries, perhaps did as much to further Jefferson's hopes for an educated citizenry as did free public schooling. Carnegie's generosity was an emblem of industry's power to improve the life of the ordinary citizen. Industrial development in the South after the Civil War made the North even richer, but it also did more to reconcile the nation than all the ideological and political pressures of Reconstruction. It is also true, of course, that industrial forces fanned imperialism, were responsible for corruption in high places, and often cruelly exploited labor. All this made for choppy seas, but somehow the American identity not only stayed afloat but seemed to become more buoyant. "The mystique of nationhood developing after the

21. *Machine in the Garden*, 349.

Civil War" drew on the "Dynamo," but it was not, according to Jones, primarily driven by its power.[22]

In contrast to Blackmur's view that Henry Adams was drawn to the industrial exhibits at the fair in 1893 because they embodied the emerging unity of American experience, Jones documented a different history. He showed that Adams actually concentrated on the architecture in Chicago and was not really fully responsive to the "Dynamo" until the Paris Exhibition of 1900. Yes, argued Jones, industrial technology was a new force in the 1890s, but it was fueled by energies that transcended its own immediate source of power. Adams was astonished by the "Dynamo" in 1900, but Jones insisted that the "Dynamo" was itself driven by an ideology of wonder more powerful than the religious passion of the "Virgin" it had superseded; a "vitalist" vision that blended the past and the present, theology and science, art and technology, and thereby embodied the true hopes of the nation at large:

> The evanescent beauty, the wonder of the Exposition, notably the Court of Honor, was what thousands remembered as long as they lived. The formal central basin was dominated by Daniel Chester French's standing statue, "The Republic," a smaller replica of which still exists in Jackson Park. It was supposed to be balanced by MacMonnies' fountain at the end of the basin, and in a sense it was, but the fountain seems to have been, at least in its main element, clumsy and ill conceived. Its principal component was an absurd ship having a pedestal with a seated figure in place of a mast and at the prow a winged figure holding out a laurel wreath to nobody in particular. (There were also four female rowers on each side of the pedestal, an effect that gave the vessel an air of either laboring forward or tipping backward; and the figure of Time was using his scythe as a rudder!) Any dissatisfaction that one might feel, however, concerning a particular statue was lost in the total impression of majesty, of harmony, of hope and futurity conceived by Burnham, Olmstead, Saint-Gaudens, and all the glorious band of associated architects, sculptors, and painters, who managed to instill into the great basin and its adjoining architecture their own passionate ideality. Calling the style classical, or Beaux-Arts, or Renaissance, or anything one likes, one could not forget this vision of an imperial country, the great offspring of republican Rome, taking shape as a White City adorned with columns and statues, colonnades and triumphal arches, made fair with stately buildings and illuminated at night by that new wonder, the electric light. Here was a mingling of the Old World and

22. HMJ, *Age of Energy,* 46.

> the New, an embodied idealism, a sense not of what the United States was but of what the United States might become. The possibilities of civic planning were made evident also, but the deeper impression of wonder is what lingered in the mind.[23]

In this eloquent passage Jones urbanely and gently mocked the clumsy progress of French's statue, but he did not permit himself the disdain of Blackmur's "trader's classicism." "The Republic" was an "absurd ship" that nevertheless sailed toward a grandeur just beyond its intellectual and aesthetic grasp. Jones painted a prose picture-poem, a "historical landscape," an ironic allegory that reminds us of his favorite German poet, Heine. Jones was convinced that the empirical ground, for all its tremors, in which American sensibility was rooted between 1865 and 1915 was precisely what enabled it to stand firm *and* to dream, to balance matter and spirit. The entire nation seemed to be captured in that picturesque and slightly absurd sculpture sailing into a landscape of wonder. Despite its monumental presumption, French's "Republic" was akin to that "tiny figure" in the foreground of an immense landscape, the archetype Jones identified with the Hudson River school. He had trusted in the ship of epic to bring him to this shore. He was now ready to disembark, he himself that tiny figure now emboldened to enter the landscape, explore its corners, and range across its expanse with a confidence born of close observation and sympathetic imagination. His own words must speak for him:

> By 1865 . . . hundreds of thousands of American feet had tramped the earth from Atlanta to the sea and from Maine to California. That generation and their successors learned that the world exists, that rain falls, that snow freezes, that wealth can be torn from the soil and out of the hills, that rivers run to bear traffic, space exists for railroads, oil to be burned, forests for making two-by-fours, electricity to be transmitted over cables and wires. Skyscrapers rose above the level land. Wealth in the period, not surprisingly, expressed itself in the acquisition of things (it is significant that most financial tycoons wanted a gold currency); and when you look at the paintings, the sculpture, the architecture, the books, you are overwhelmed by the conviction of their creators that the world is as we see it and that the business of style is to be a mode of representing things as they are, sometimes a little bit heightened, sometimes a little imagined, but always as physical fidelity. We, who mainly project our queer images of life rather than register actuality, we who

23. Ibid., 144, 256–57.

live in contorted and private universes of our own devising, cannot understand this emergence out of the chaos of war and the clouds of imagination into the daylight of physics and chemistry, industry and invention, of a way to picture things as they exist. Formerly a problem of the soul; now flesh and blood, stone and steel, meat and drink, landscape and building. This was the great transformation in style these fruitful years accomplished.[24]

24. Ibid., 17–18.

8

Humanism Abides: A Polemical Conclusion

"Too many writers talk as if men exist for books." This assertion, redolent of Jones's passionate trust in the ideals of *Paidea*—education as the nurse of perfection—reminds us that he never saw literature as an end in itself. It was the instrument of a higher purpose. "Culture," he wrote one year after the publication of *Revolution and Romanticism,* "belongs to character." Ten years earlier he had specified what *character* meant in relation to the duties of a teacher of the humanities: "The primary duty of the humanist is not to follow fashion or to heap up historical lore, but is to consider fashion critically in the light of historical learning, and, achieving a responsible philosophy, to teach such wisdom as he can. I believe this duty falls equally upon those who teach in the public schools and those who teach in colleges and universities." Jones did not question the uniqueness of art, but he never believed that art could totalize reality in its own image. In 1952 he wrote: "Art is autonomous only as a province within the larger empire of human history and of human experience." A Derridean reading of this sentence might argue that Jones's use of the word *empire* to characterize "human history" belies the necessity of the province to remain loyal. Empires tyrannize. Jones's language gives him away. The liberal in him has overcome the stuffy humanist and has endorsed the autonomy of art in the very act of questioning it.[1]

What happens next in a poststructuralist reading, however, is precisely what Jones warned against when he insisted that men do not "exist for books." The language of art presumes on its autonomy to imperialize history and experience; the province rebels and becomes a tyrant. As Jean Howard reflected on the essence of New Historicism, "One imagines a complex textualized universe in which literature participates in historical process and in the political management of reality."[2] One is tempted to practice a bit of deconstruction on the postdeconstructionist mentality exhibited in *this* sentence. If we contrast Howard's words (textualized universe . . . participates . . . process . . . management) with Jones's (duty . . . historical learning . . . responsible philosophy . . . teach . . . wisdom), we cannot help but remark on the dehumanizing effect of the former. Instead of describing literature as a vehicle of liberation, these words suggest that it has joined hands with determinisms that preclude freedom. To "manage" reality may provide the illusion of freedom, but it is, at best, to stand in relation to reality in a manner that reduces perception and imagination to an efficiency of process with a taint of manipulation; and "*political* management" of "reality" embarrasses the ambition of politics while naively offending the mystery of reality.

What a postmodernist sensibility may forget is that if indeed we do live in a "textualized universe," the legendary burning of the library in Alexandria should have been a greater disaster than the flood. Noah's menagerie was an absolute necessity; without it, no humanity would follow. The texts lost in the Egyptian fire were lost, but others followed. When Hitler burned books, some said he was burning civilization. Heine wrote that when books are burned, people come next. The burning of books may prepare for the burning of people, but they are not equivalent. In order to destroy his own culture, Hitler had to burn people. There is no substitute for the "human cry." The greatest literary minds have always understood this and have often been vehement in

1. HMJ, review of *On Native Grounds,* 5–6. "Humanism Today," 375. "History and the Contemporary," in *History and the Contemporary,* 18; previously published in *Teachers College Record* 64 (May 1963): 625–36.

2. "The New Historicism in Renaissance Studies," 25.

their refusal to provide textuality with the metaphysical authority that they have felt was grounded in their own humanity. One thinks of Tolstoy, who rejected his own masterpieces because their textuality cut them off from the people as a whole. In his recently published biography, Nicholas Boyle notes that Goethe's "secularized religion" never succumbed to the textual urgency of "German theology secularizing itself into philosophy." While "practically all of Goethe's literary contemporaries became at some point or in some respect tributary to one or other of the religious philosophies that resulted . . . no orthodoxy, old or new, not Kant nor Fichte nor Schelling nor Hegel could seduce Goethe, not even in his youth the deistical Enlightenment of Voltaire or Lessing, or Basedow. His secularized religion remained what it had been before secularization—a wholly, even obsessively, personal piety: *his* relation with *his* heavenly Father, and no one else's."[3]

We remember Jones's Spenglerian interest in Faustian man and the importance he placed on will as a force that transcended structures or rational models of all sorts in the nineteenth century. The discrete language and passionate nominalism of contemporary literary criticism would have puzzled him, not just because of the jargon but primarily because of the impersonality of the "textualized universe" this criticism inhabits. For all of his distrust of irrationality, Jones was never persuaded that impersonal objectivity was synonymous with a rational humanism: "The humanist sometimes worships at the false shrine of objectivity. Great scholars and great scientists are not like this. It was not thus that George Lyman Kittredge or John Livingston Lowes or Karl Vietor or Jules Jusserand did their writing. If you cut their books, those books will bleed. Such men mastered materials; they did not let materials master them." Despite his distaste for the way Freudianism had somehow valorized the irrational in modern literature, Jones had great respect for Freud himself, whose mastery of a wide range of learning had revolutionized our rational grasp of subjectivity. "It is apparently idle to point out that Sigmund Freud was a man of great historical culture whose thinking was strongly influenced by the Bible, by Goethe, and by Darwin, and that, far from seeking to destroy the rational basis of culture, he thought he was enriching and fortifying the long Western tradition."[4]

3. *The Poetry of Desire (1749–1790),* vol. 1 of *Goethe: The Poet and the Age,* 191.
4. HMJ, *Autobiography,* 247; *History and the Contemporary,* 18.

"Great historical culture" was Jones's ideal, and all his life he believed that to grow in learning was its own reward, that a profound grasp of what had been judged great in the past could raise the sincere humanist to a level of insight that would speak for culture. To accept the past's judgments and determinations of greatness did not preclude one's own right or will to evaluation, but not to know the past rendered the judgments of the present puerile. Unlike F. R. Leavis, Jones did not see in tradition a binding moral imperative, but rather a model one would be foolish to ignore. "The humanist," he believed, "is always in some degree a historian of culture as culture has expressed itself in some durable form."[5]

We have seen how Jones was propelled by his need to be both "encyclopedic" and "selective" and how the former legitimized the latter. The current running between these two ways of thinking and working energized a power in Jones that seems all too weak in today's literary discourse; what I have in mind is the power to evaluate, to say with conviction that something is "good" or "bad." A reader glancing back at the many passages I have quoted from Jones's different writings must note the robust emphasis of his tone, the sureness of his commentary. If he was slow to generalize, he was all the more resolute when he did so. His evaluative specialty lay in calling contemporary dismissal of traditional writers to account; when he moved to rescue Cooper or Longfellow, he did it by forcing the contemporary reader to set aside the green glasses of his own time and don the spectacles of the past. He admired scholarship that provided this kind of intellectual liberation. "I have found few essays on the development of any American poet more illuminating than Charvat's studies of the relation of Henry Wadsworth Longfellow to his publishers and his public. It compelled me to re-examine all the traditional presuppositions and prejudices that have obscured the genuine achievements of one of the great prosodists in American letters."[6]

In *The Classic,* Frank Kermode explores the problematics of literary greatness and uses a subtle historical argument to distinguish between the old and the new conception of classic. The old is Virgilian and tied to attitudes of empire and eternity; the new embraces change,

5. *Scholarship, Novelty, and Teaching: An Address in Memory of the Late William Charvat,* 20.

6. Ibid., 31–32.

plurality, and secularization: "The modern classic . . . offers itself only to readings which are encouraged by its failure to give a definitive account of itself. Unlike the old classic, which was expected to provide answers, this one poses a virtually infinite set of questions." Kermode, whose learning is certainly as great as Jones's, alludes to Jones's citing of the Greek and Roman "public iconography" of the early United States but maintains that "the imperial confidence of Americans" eventually gave way "especially in the North" to "a new past which was not classical but Hebraic. This did not alter the deep-seated conviction of an imperial destiny, but it gave it a missionary quality." When Jones concluded that both Benjamin Franklin and Jonathan Edwards shared the heart of American being, he was asserting an oxymoronic reality about America that, as we have already noted, he saw in epic terms. Kermode also recognizes the typological direction of American consciousness from Locke through Edwards to Emerson, but, like Henry Adams, although with a lighter touch, he rejects the model of epic transcendence and, following Hegel, ultimately locates the modern classic in the hermeneutic splendor and chaos of tropological tragedy.[7] Kermode sees literary history the same way as Hayden White sees historiography. What becomes clearer with time is that the subtler our hermeneutics becomes, the richer our variety of "interpretation" and reading becomes, the more our entire critical and historical enterprise finds itself removed from evaluation. We have wrapped ourselves in the text to such a degree that we now are beginning to confuse the text with reality. By insisting that the purpose of literature is to engage culture, Jones gave literature heroic work to do, work that could be evaluated by criteria that resided elsewhere than in literature itself.

From late nineteenth-century aestheticism to deconstruction, literature has been understood as autotelic; it need not answer to any other gods than its own sacred meaning—or meaninglessness. For Oscar Wilde, life imitated art, a metaphysical boast that put Apollo on the Olympian throne; for Derrida, life cannot escape art, and literary art is, alas, mired in linguistic indeterminacy. The end result of a century of often brilliant descriptive literary criticism seems to be an intellectual impasse in which various skepticisms emanating from anthropology and psychoanalysis, as well as from linguistics and social criti-

7. Frank Kermode, *The Classic: Literary Images of Permanence and Change,* 114, 87, 90.

cism, are jockeying for positions of authority in what many call, with some charity, a pluralistic consensus. What we have now are many different voices demonstrating in many different ways how we *cannot* know the object as it really is. Language, gender, repression, custom—or combinations of all four—become the agents of descriptive theorization on the centrifugal forces at work in literature.

For Jones the human cry preceded the literary voice. If life did at times imitate art, it was because both bad and good art have a way of sticking to memory and staining feeling—not because imagination has a metaphysical authority over reason. In great art the relationship between the two is reciprocal, as Wordsworth understood when he called imagination "reason in its most exalted mood." When Jones praised the closing lines of *The Prelude*, he emphasized Wordsworth's sense of duty, his awareness of the other-than-self in the very act of celebrating the self:

> In sum, Wordsworth has traced "the history of a Poet's mind," knows that he has been called upon to do the work of genius, and has a duty to other men to
>
> Instruct them how the mind of man becomes
> A thousand times more beautiful than the earth
> On which he dwells, above this frame of things
>
> . . . .
>
> In beauty exalted, as it is itself
> Of quality and fabric more divine.
>
> In his dark striving Wordsworth, always conscious of the right way, has in fact drawn near the abode where the eternal are. There are hundreds of unsolved riddles in *The Prelude*, but one point is clear: men may rise on stepping stones of their dead selves to higher things.[8]

"Higher things" are not necessarily religious in an orthodox Christian sense, but they are higher than and beyond art. They provide the "high" of Arnold's "high seriousness" and, if nothing else, enable the reader to make evaluative judgments. Jones mined so much cultural ore that he never lost his sense of what was culturally possible in the service of transcendent values. He chose the epic path—as scholar, critic, and historian—because it enabled him to be generous in taste and firm in judgment. His idea of the classic did not wander from imperial order to subjective chaos; his idea of the classic was both

8. *Revolution and Romanticism*, 449.

more liberal and less relative than that. But it *was* a norm. Jones was at his best in defining that norm when he talked about the humanities:

> The humanities are, then, a group of subjects devoted to the study of man as a being other than a biological product and different from a social or sociological entity. They make certain assumptions about human nature and about history. First, they assume that man lives in a dimension lying beyond science and the social sciences. Second, they assume that his profound sense of individuation is one of the most important things about him. Third, they assume that the better traits of humanity, or, if one likes, the enduring elements of human nature, find typical expression in philosophy, in literature, in language, and in the arts, and that history is both the way by which these expressions are preserved and one of the principal modes of interpreting the meaning of these expressions to and in contemporary life. Historically, since they sprang from ancient Greece and Rome, humane studies antecede theology and are not primarily conditioned by theological considerations, but like theology they aim at a better state of being for man. Fourth, the purpose of the humanities is refining and maturing the individual who studies them sympathetically and intelligently, evidence of refinement and maturation being given by increased sympathy with and understanding of philosophy and the arts in past and present time and increased sympathy with and understanding of man not only as he is but as he has been. Humane studies tend to concentrate upon individual development rather more than upon social judgment, and differ from science in this regard also, since science properly seeks to eliminate the personal equation. Incidental to these several aims, humane learning also creates, as it were, methods and disciplines of its own, such as intellectual history.[9]

This manifesto appears in the early pages of his book published in 1959, which Jones later described as follows: "I have written and published a good many books, but I think I have been responsible for none more directly aimed at American values than is *One Great Society.* 'There is,' wrote Wordsworth, 'one great society alone on earth: / The noble Living and the noble Dead.'" *One Great Society* represents the culmination of Jones's work for the American Council of Learned Societies, which he chaired from 1955 to 1959 and which he almost single-handedly saved from bankruptcy and cultural irrelevance. Readers will remember that Jones convened a special group of scholars, scientists, and industrialists to provide information and ideas for a report to the nation on the status and purpose of the humanities in American society. This "commission" included such distinguished

9. *One Great Society,* 17.

names as Whitney J. Oates, classicist; Charles W. Hendel, philosopher; Robert Oppenheimer, "philosophical scientist"; and nine other worthies from academia, theology, the performing arts, and the corporate world. Jones was elected to chair the group, and the group, when they had concluded their deliberations, authorized him to write a report. *One Great Society: Humane Learning in the United States,* a labor of love, was his parting gift to the ACLS. "The Commission, desirous of a unified report, instructed its Chairman to speak for the whole body, though not necessarily to reflect every difference of opinion among the members of the Commission. This he has tried to do."[10]

What has happened to his legacy? Does the ACLS still speak for the humanities in the same way that Jones did when he galvanized scholars and intellectuals some thirty-five years ago to reaffirm the importance of humane letters? Does the organization he rescued still believe in his agenda for the rescue of humanism? "Like theology they [the humanities] aim at a better state of being for man." Jones linked the ethical dimension of the humanities to their passion for general knowledge and deep respect for history: "The humanities depend for their very existence upon perspective in time, so that history is the essence of their being." Great literature stands in relief when the reader has general knowledge and historical awareness, and evaluation is activated, primarily, by these two things. Jones felt that writers could be "wrong" (that is, ethically confused) when they lacked the general knowledge and historical awareness that should have made them, and should make the reader, conscious of their weakness as writers in the humanities:

> The critical question is not whether the novel is now better or worse under Freud and Jung than it was when Cooper and Hawthorne wrote, but whether the image of American life in the novel endorses or questions or denies our two great original premises: first, that an enduring republic can be founded on human nature; and second, that the arts in this republic will support and nourish this particular representative system and this particular democratic society. If the novelists are now right about human nature, then the philosophic postulates in which we began may be wildly wrong; and if the philosophical postulates are right, the novelists may be, if not wrong, at least obsessed with a wrong headed value system.[11]

10. HMJ, *Autobiography,* 257; *One Great Society,* ix.
11. *One Great Society,* 12; "American Studies in Higher Education," 19.

Categorical identification with too discrete a way of knowing (for example, Freud and Jung thirty-five years ago, deconstruction today) is the result, felt Jones, of a "mistaken attitude toward *knowledge*":

> Contemporary belief in the superiority of *expertise,* whether it be embodied in the radio repairman or in those charged with launching an artificial satellite, overshadows the concept of general knowledge. Moreover, a misunderstanding of science leads many to think that "scientific method" can be applied to almost any department of life. When, for example, a "scientific" study of ethics proves that all moral judgments are relative, it is next inferred that *all* value judgments must therefore be relative also.

Jones's connection of the lure of expertise with early psychoanalysis and scientism speaks for the paradigms of the late 1950s. Today the relativizing of value judgments has its roots, as we have discussed in earlier chapters, in combinations of linguistics, anthropology, new varieties of psychoanalytical theory, feminism, Marxism, multiculturalism, and, of course, postmodern historiography. The very fact that the relativizing of values has such a long list of various kinds of expertise in its service (and my list is certainly not exhaustive) suggests that Jones was right in thinking that the humanities in the modern world, particularly in America, pined for the authority of *Sachlichkeit,* for an objectivity in cultural discourse that would rival the quantitative and statistical weight of the physical and social sciences.[12]

In 1989 the American Council of Learned Societies published an occasional paper entitled *Speaking for the Humanities,* which represents nearly a 180-degree turn from what Jones had emphasized thirty years earlier. It is true that the editor and writers (George Levine and Peter Brooks, Jonathan Culler, Marjorie Garber, E. Ann Kaplan, Catharine R. Stimpson) of this pamphlet did not see themselves in debate with Jones, at least not directly. Their intention was to confront what they perceived as an extremely conservative, even reactionary, alliance that was headed by the Republican establishment, specifically the former secretary of education William Bennett and the former head of the National Endowment for the Humanities Lynne Cheney, who was also the wife of George Bush's secretary of defense, and was supported by journals like *The American Scholar, The New Criterion, Commentary,* and *The New Republic,* and by scholars like Allan Bloom,

12. *One Great Society,* 71–72.

whose "disturbingly popular *The Closing of the American Mind* seems . . . to attribute major moral and social changes in America to the failure of the humanities to insist on and teach the great philosophical tradition from Plato through Rousseau." *Speaking for the Humanities* insists that all of the above "tend to overlook those aspects of the humanities that have been attempting to respond creatively and responsibly to the evolution of basic research and to contemporary social and cultural change."[13]

Howard Mumford Jones in his very last years was given to dyspeptic conversation about the vacillation of the Carter administration and even indulged in some patriotic breastbeating when expressing hopes that Ronald Reagan might reactivate American energy. I suspect Jones was revisiting his lifelong affection for Theodore Roosevelt and indulging in visions of an American savior, visions he had articulated ten years earlier with subtle historical insight in what many feel was his best book. Even as Jones celebrated Roosevelt's heroic "pragmatism," he could not ignore his faults:

> His preachments of a simplistic morality do not now appeal. We have passed beyond his boyish belief that manly sports would save the nation; we do not care for his simple-minded excursions into literary criticism, the fine arts, racial qualities, and the meaning of history. His activism of the "Damn-the-torpedoes!-Go-ahead" school seems inapplicable, and we are troubled by the discrepancy between his denunciation of corporations and his pragmatic insistence that there were good trusts and bad ones.[14]

13. George Levine, ed., *Speaking for the Humanities,* 2, 4.

14. *Age of Energy,* 394. Jones concludes his discussion in *Age of Energy* with a "Plutarchian" portrait of Theodore Roosevelt: "Lincoln aside, we have had no man in the White House since Andrew Jackson's time of Theodore Roosevelt's extraordinary energy, range, and curiosity. . . . Not only is Oscar Handlin justified in calling him the first modern chief executive, but it is also true, I think, that in Roosevelt the Age of Energy focused upon a chief magistrate who embodied its restlessness, its ambition, its curiosity, its extraordinary faith in activism rather than in contemplation, its inconsistencies, and, above all, its ceaseless search of American life for what I may fairly call a pragmatic sanction that would validate the activities of a modern state. . . . Roosevelt was a man curiously reminiscent of the Renaissance, a *uomo universale,* a hunter, a sportsman, a historian, a soldier, an administrator, a social and political reformer, a moralist, a literary critic, an explorer, and above all, a man who carried out the principles of Castiglione's *Il Cortegiano,* for Roosevelt seized upon his puny boyish body and his defective eyesight and by the sheer power of will transformed himself into the tireless human dynamo admired by John Morley. One of his most characteris-

To rehearse Jones on Roosevelt is to bring out Jones's liberalism. His appreciation for heroic individualism and his belief in the dignity of the "human cry" place him in opposition to postmodernism without branding him a reactionary or inflexible traditionalist. Long before contemporary feminists or multiculturalists discovered gender and non-Western culture, Jones had championed Willa Cather (*The Bright Medusa,* 1952) and Ellen Glasgow (who considered the Joneses among her dearest friends) and had urged the study of Asian civilization in general education courses (*Education and World Tragedy,* 1946). And certainly no important American humanist was more tuned to the connections between popular culture and politics and the life of the mind.

The truth is that for all their egalitarian pronouncements, the scholars who speak for the humanities through the ACLS today are deeply estranged from any general or universal value system that might connect them with their fellow human beings. They valorize academic specialization with such self-assurance ("general significance only develops from specialized and particularized research") that one wants to read them Jones's admonition on the fallacy of scientific "expertise" as a model for "knowing" in the humanities. Tzvetan Todorov chastised the writers of the pamphlet on precisely this point:

> They declare that "specialization makes thought possible." This is an outrageous claim. It implies, among other things, that outside of universities people do not think. (But this is consistent with the elitism elsewhere in this defense: such-and-such a book is "disturbingly popular," problems are inevitably "more complicated than the popular interpretation allows.") To justify this stance, we are given an analogy with the natural sciences.[15]

We remember that Jones insisted that people do not live for books, that he never succumbed to the authority of the "selective" over the "encyclopedic," that he could distinguish between a "disinterested" and an "interested" position. He could recognize the lasting value of

---

tic performances occurred when, disgusted with 'softness' in army officers, he rode ninety-eight miles in one day to show that it could be done. 'I cannot praise,' wrote Milton, 'a fugitive and cloistered virtue, unexercised and unbreathed, that never sallies out.' I suggest that Roosevelt exemplified an important component of sixteenth- and seventeenth-century humanism" (394–95).

15. Levine, *Speaking for the Humanities,* 5; Tzvetan Todorov, "Crimes against Humanities," 28.

Arnold's idea of culture at the same time that he condemned his snobbism and class prejudices. Jones's learning told him that there were men, women, and ideas that had found "the abode where the eternal are" and men, women, and ideologies that had not. Idea and ideology could, of course, struggle for supremacy in the same mind. Like Arnold, everyone may fail his or her values. But the ideas that inform our values do not inform the same knowing and being that inhabit our ideologies. An idea stands out in the landscape of history in a way that an ideology cannot. Pound's idea of poetic integrity, for all his insistence that it represented a new realism in image and sound, was still in touch with what Jones identified as the "belief of Winckelmann or Goethe that art is ideal form."[16] Pound's idea of poetry eventually drowned in the ideological frenzy of his politics; the first was a cultural achievement, the second a moral embarrassment.

The authors of *Speaking for the Humanities* maintain, "The best contemporary work in the humanities strives to make clear both its critique of the ideologies of previous work, and its own inevitable ideological blindspots." To see the humanities in this way is to condemn them to endless bricolage, a kind of fine tuning in which all the various mechanical parts of that monster we call humane culture are constantly repaired, replaced, or phased out as irrelevant, offensive, or politically incorrect. Shakespeare, Milton, and Wordsworth had blind spots (in theology and politics), but a close inspection of these failures in perception rarely raises the ideas that make them great poets. When Blake said that Milton was of the devil's party without knowing it, he was not citing an "ideological blindspot." The pamphlet writers refuse to grant values any meaning divorced from their localized or anthropological expression; hence, the humanities are subsumed by the social sciences. It becomes sheer folly, a kind of metaphysical naïveté, to believe, as Jones said was a fundamental characteristic of the humanities, that they are "a group of subjects devoted to the study of man as a being other than a biological product and different from a social or sociological entity." Quite the contrary, insist the writers of *Speaking for the Humanities:* "At its best, contemporary humanistic thinking does not peddle ideology, but rather attempts to sensitize us to the presence of ideology in our work, and to its capacity to delude us into promoting as universal values that in

16. *The Scholar as American*, 4.

fact belong to one nation, one social class, one sect."[17] Were he still with us, Howard Mumford Jones would certainly wonder to what purpose he had saved the ACLS.

Tzvetan Todorov, in his review, raps the knuckles of the pamphlet writers with exactly the kind of "ideas" that Jones would have forced them to confront. I quote Todorov at length because he sounds ideas that contemporary theorists would prefer to dismiss as fatuous. The very resonance of his remarks has the effect of removing the dust from Jones's stubborn liberal humanism:

> The distinctive trait of human beings is not only to have specific motives, but to be capable of surmounting them. Everyone (except Callicles) knows the difference between what is advantageous and what is just. The fact that algebra was discovered by the Arabs does not make it any less true in China. The fact that declarations of human rights were drawn up in Europe does not mean these rights need not be respected in South Africa. And the possibility of consensus, the aspiration to universality, is obviously much closer to the democratic ideal than are the philosophies that present the world as given over to irreducible interests, to a war among races, nations, classes, or sexes.
>
> The very frequency with which authoritative voices are invoked in the ACLS pamphlet suggests that its authors are betting on the ignorance of their readers. Yet it is not true that all 'dominant,' 'distinguished,' and 'powerful' professors agree on these matters. The cognitive and moral relativism at the basis of this doctrine proceeds from Nietzsche or, differently, from Marx. A great many thinkers take exception to this 'consensus.' There are those who propound a dogmatic truth (Christian thinkers, for example, but also from a different angle, the Marxists themselves). And there are those who maintain that truth is neither a dogma nor a chimera, that it is, rather, the horizon of dialogue, the regulating principle of exchange (these thinkers range from Kant to Habermas and beyond). Eliminating such disagreements out of hand hardly instantiates the 'pluralism' of which the authors of *Speaking for the Humanities* boast. It is proof only of their uniformity. They seem to practice dogmatic skepticism.[18]

Todorov's closing phrase, *dogmatic skepticism,* is, as cited earlier, Denis Donoghue's choice of words to define deconstruction. For Jones such relentless doubting was not only scientism at its worst but also irrationalist persuasion and therefore essentially anti-intellectual and definitely hostile to the moral values that make culture possible. What

17. *Speaking for the Humanities,* 11.
18. "Crimes against Humanities," 29.

would have saddened him greatly is that this kind of thinking is now allied with social reform and the championing of the ethnic traditions of minorities in the United States. Jones would have rejoiced over *scholarly* multiculturalism and would have been entitled to boast that it was simply the latest version of "American Studies," the movement in American culture studies that he himself had helped launch in the 1930s. But he would have scoffed at the notion that "tribalism" was an end in itself; that, as the current ACLS leadership would have it, significant ideas were seriously identified with their ideological or tribal manifestation. Jones believed that to recognize the greatest achievements of non-European cultures was merely another way of discovering the humanistic ascendancy of aesthetic and ethical power in the creations of great artists and thinkers in all cultures. The "human cry" was not restricted to the West's idea of individualism or philosophies of the will. Jones was not loath to correct such a bias no matter in whom he found it: "Even so good a critic of art as Bernard Berenson seems unable to make this readjustment, declaring at the close of *Aesthetics and History* that the only true tradition in art originates in the Mediterranean world."[19]

Variety of cultures, no matter how interesting, is, however, no guarantee of their humanistic significance. To think in such terms is merely to indulge the American proclivity to confuse quantitative representation with knowledge, to enumerate cultures rather than evaluate them. The current ethical passion devoted to multiculturalizing the curriculum may have a political and social validity as a form of inspirational "civism," but it must strain to lay claim to humanistic authority. It certainly cannot do so unless it holds the cultures it examines to the standards established by the fine arts and philosophic thought of the civilized past. Pluralism in politics is sound democratic doctrine, but pluralism does not approximate humanism until it becomes cosmopolitanism. Democracy can survive without cosmopolitanism, but an ethnically diverse internationalist power that, like the United States, frowns on isolationism cannot achieve stability *and* culture without the cosmopolitan spirit.

America is forever torn between two creeds: individualism and conformity. They change costumes, but never leave the stage. Jones had a keen sense for the drama *and* the absurdity of this conflict; he

19. *One Great Society*, 168.

saw that our inability to ease this tension prevented the American intellect from understanding "the nature and limits of *social action*":

> Traditionally, America is the land of rugged individualism, although during the pioneer phase the necessity for communal activities and the push toward conformity were evident. During the post–Civil War period, while spokesmen for business, industry, and public affairs continued to praise individualism (the so-called "Protestant Ethic"), the need to assimilate millions of immigrants, social pressures in our mushrooming cities, and the astonishing efflorescence of the social sciences combined with other forces to make social adjustment desirable. In the twentieth century psychological testing, personal engineering, concepts of group organization, group research, group dynamics and the like, the theory that "co-operation carries its own ethic," and, negatively, fear of personal, domestic, social, and emotional insecurity have further limited the area of individual action. The McCarthy episode helped to substitute for stick-to-itiveness the cynical twentieth-century saw: "Don't stick your neck out." In education the fallacy takes shape in the assumption that engineers, or scientists, or businessmen, or teachers are "products" of "training" and that in times of stress like the post-Sputnik era education can be speeded up to "deliver" more and better scientists. Meantime, every commencement speaker greets the class as leaders of tomorrow, in periods of political tension angry editorials demand "leadership," and, always, enterprises as variegated as publishing, sports, science, industry, and interior decorating cry aloud for more "talent." Another ritualistic demand is for "men of imagination." But the incompatibility of simultaneously demanding originality and requiring conformity is clear, and the effect is to weaken decision-making. Since responsibility can be referred to a committee, an adviser, a cabinet, a staff, a sales conference, or an opinion analysis, why stick your neck out? If you are loyal, why also be original? There are, of course, vigorous individuals in American life, but our interest here is in cultural imbalance.[20]

We have in this long paragraph the familiar Jones signatures: binary structure (originality and conformity) and the "epic catalogues" of series just a little longer than necessary. These, accompanied by the long historical view (from pioneer days to the organization man), are the inscriptions of his "encyclopedic" style. The counterbalancing "selectivity" is evident in the moral judgment Jones is making on the failures of "social action" in the late 1950s, when McCarthyism was

20. Ibid., 72–73.

making a mockery of individualism and education was conforming to the sacred and war-tested ethos of the assembly line.

It would seem that America in the 1990s continues to suffer from a "misunderstanding of the nature and limits of *social action*," and, as if to underscore the universality of Jones's insight, the problem continues to be centered in our wavering between individualism and conformity and the resulting cultural uncertainty. Multiculturalism berates the injustices of the past but at the same time reduces the cosmopolitan history of culture to a tribalist anthropology in order to highlight contemporary reality and dismiss the past, where culture breathes as deeply as injustice resonates. This war on history not only blinds the present to the epic efforts of modern culture to rise above the anthropologically given, but it also does great personal harm to the social groups it presumes to save. We are forcing individuals among our ethnic citizenry into a group conformity that is proffered as a form of liberation. We cannot promise them a cultural enlightenment within their tribal life just because we excuse them from feeling the need to assimilate into our conforming national society. The "human cry," to which Jones tuned his theories of cultural history, yearns for a liberation beyond tribalism.

In 1942, one of the darkest years of World War II, Jones was called to Wellesley College to deliver the Phi Beta Kappa Address. He entitled it "Tribalism." Remembering, perhaps, his displeasure with Wilson's ambassador, Walter Hines Page, for exaggerating America's indebtedness to English culture in order to whip up pro-British sentiment during World War I, Jones used the occasion to attack propaganda that was pleading, once again, the "supremacy of the Anglo-Saxons" and arguing that mainly *because* of Anglo-Saxon superiority it was the duty of free men everywhere, including "South" Ireland, to support Britain against Hitler. "I am not, and I have never been, an Anglophobe," Jones reminded his audience. "I make my living by teaching the literature of England, and I know something of what Great Britain has contributed to the wealth, the culture, the stability, and the happiness of the world." Having smoothed the way, Jones went on to the heart of the matter:

> When the tribe thinks it is superior to the human family, the result is tribalism. There is a vague feeling among us that only the enemy suffers from tribalism. We have to thank the Nazis for the most outrageous form of this fallacy, to be sure. The monstrous Nordic myth, a myth

> without basis in history, in anthropology, in philology, or in natural science, reveals by its colossal crudity all that is fallacious in the idea of tribalism. If we are ever to have enduring peace, we must destroy Nazi tribalism and all the so-called philosophy which supports it. . . . But we cannot win the war only to substitute for Nazi tribalism a more genteel tribalism of our own.

Jones traces America's "genteel tribalism," Anglo-Saxonism, to its Victorian origins in works like John Mitchell Kemble's *The Saxons in England* (1849) and the "lectures of E. A. Freeman at Johns Hopkins University and the Lowell Institute in 1881." The glorification of "Anglo-Saxon stock" as the driving force behind everything that provides "strength and stability and character to our government" struck Jones as social and historical nonsense: "In Wisconsin, where I grew up, the postmaster was named Skaar, the Congressman was named Esch, the Senator was named La Follette, the president of the university was named Van Hise, and the creator of the so-called 'Wisconsin idea' was named McCarthy. We thought we had a pretty stable government, but there wasn't an Anglo-Saxon in the lot."[21] Jones exposes the same unwarranted trust in "conformity" that he attacked some fifteen years later in *One Great Society;* to collectivize one's subjectivity in a racial, ethnic, or social myth is a poor man or woman's cultural history.

Everything that Jones had learned about the plenitude of history, the way it always eluded attempts to categorize its nature by identifying it too exclusively with any one group or ideology, persuaded him that the lifeline of culture was the thinking, feeling individual who reached beyond his tribe. His long debate with Perry Miller was rooted in that scholar's insistence that Puritanism was the defining idea in American life. What this kind of totalizing ignored was the fact that the thinking and feeling Puritan, from Emerson to James, in his reaching for culture inevitably found himself involved with either French or German ideas that questioned the core of Puritanism. The truth is that every idea, when it becomes too closely identified with a group's program or embodiment, risks becoming a mere ideology. Postmodernism, from Barthes to Foucault and beyond, is convinced that we do not have the luxury of separating what we are from the groups in which we live and the languages that we speak. We are promised liberation down the road if only we are tough-minded enough to learn

21. HMJ, "Tribalism," in *Ideas in America,* 224–25, 228.

how impoverished our so-called individualism really is, how fated we are. But there is much bad faith in this promise because those who make it delight too much in the demonstration of our bondage. When the group and conformity to the group are given metaphysical sanction, tyranny is in the wings:

> The difference between National Socialism and all previous systems, particularly the system it is now conquering, is that its starting point is the community, not the individual. This gives a very different character to all our social ideas. What I mean when I say war, or society, or economics, or political philosophy, all these things suddenly appear from a different angle. We do not see these things from the point of view of the individual, but from that of the community.

So said Joseph Goebbels.[22]

Jones carried his attack on "genteel tribalism" in that speech he gave fifty years ago to a conclusion that would certainly warm the hearts of many multiculturalists today:

> If the Chinese, clinging to their immemorial culture, can yet profit from the traditions of the West, cannot we, clinging to the traditions of the Occident, learn profitable things from the culture of the East? Until we can learn to take the point of view that Plato has no monopoly of wisdom nor Aristotle of intellect; that, however influential the ideas of Mr. T. S. Eliot may be, they cannot compare in importance or influence with the ideas of Siddhartha Gautama, known as Buddha; until we can humble ourselves to learn that there are cultures and traditions, literature and wisdom, art and morality older and richer, perhaps even wiser, than our own—until we can remake our thought about history and humanity in some such terms as these, we cannot reach the height of our great opportunity.
>
> As I see it, the problem before Western education is how, while we cling to what is sound in national traditions, we can begin to think and act not merely as Americans, not merely as Europeans, but as members of the human race. I might remark of the requirement of courses in American history that if they return to the wisdom of the founding fathers they will help us, but only then; and I might remark of the requirement of a general

22. Joseph Goebbels, "Der Krieg als Weltanschauungskampf" (The war as a battle for a world outlook; Berlin, ca. 1944), in Joachim Remak, ed., *The Nazi Years: A Documentary History,* 40. If the connection between Nazism and certain aspects of postmodernism seems far-fetched or, perhaps, an irresponsible deepening of the de Man controversy, the reader is urged to look at a book that came to my attention only after I had completed the present study. See David H. Hirsch, *The Deconstruction of Literature: Criticism after Auschwitz,* 143–65, 255–68.

> course in the humanities that everything depends upon the points of reference we select. We can be crippled by these requirements or we can be enriched. We can be enriched, however, only if we return to the great eighteenth century concept, important for the last time in that century, of universal humanity. It is significant that the word "race" does not appear in the Declaration of Independence or the Constitution of the United States.

Catharine Stimpson, one of the framers of the statement in the ACLS pamphlet, made the following defense of multiculturalism while speaking on a panel called "The Idea of the University" at a symposium, "The Changing Culture of the University," sponsored by *The Partisan Review* in 1991:

> Multiculturalism is not a narcissistic retreat with one's ethnic or racial peers from the demands of the classroom or the polis. Multiculturalism is the recognition that we live, nationally and internationally, with many cultures, defined both anthropologically and aesthetically. Each has its meaning to its inhabitants. These cultures interact, intersect, collide, influence each other. Our task is to understand these zones of interaction and to articulate national and international unities. In the United States, the Constitution and the Bill of Rights provide a national unity. In so doing, we will be pluralistic, but we will be fearful of a pluralism that declares, "I am a pluralist but have the omniscience to judge all others."[23]

Jones and Stimpson seem to want the same thing, an openness to and tolerance of the "other." Just what the "other" is, however, and how one gets there, is another matter. For Jones the heart of a culture was its historically realized humanity; and this, significantly, is not something societies can exchange through some kind of group action at a given moment in time. What we can do, as individuals, is recognize the greatness of thought and art produced by great minds drawn from another culture's history. The resulting sense of discovery fires our imaginations and frees us from the illusion of our own tribal superiority. Passed on from mind to mind, ideas external to the tribe can change it from within. All of this suggests the kind of extended consciousness and moral transformation that we have discussed at some length as being central to epic. The American experience of the Enlightenment enabled a tribe, argued Jones, to transcend its paro-

23. HMJ, "Tribalism," in *Ideas in America*, 236; Stimpson, "The Changing Culture of the University," 337–38.

chial nature and look toward a universal ideal. In suppressing the tribal particular, America entered history and became a culture. A culture must resonate, Jones wrote, with its own historical self-discovery. In direct refutation of Hegel, Jones was telling us to make sure we know what our true "story" is and to retell it with bardic authority over and over again. We cannot reach out to the human race unless we take our bearings from our own cosmopolitan sightings in historical seas.

Catharine Stimpson concedes that tribes should "interact," but she is far more concerned with preserving the integrity and rights of tribes than with validating a transcendent idea of culture. She, of course, does not use the word *tribe* and would probably resent my using it to equate what she means by *culture*. It is revealing, however, that she links "multiculturalism" with "recognition" of "cultures, defined both anthropologically and aesthetically." Jones would question the bracketing of ethical and historical definitions of culture. Whereas "aesthetic" concepts of culture were grounded in ethics and history up until the later nineteenth century, it is quite true that modernism is much more comfortable with stressing the connection between aesthetics and anthropology; one has only to review the stories of expressionism, surrealism, and all forms of psychoanalytical and myth criticism to support such a contention. In other words, the humanist legacy of a "universal humanity," Jones's creed, becomes threatening as a totalizing doctrine when it presumes to act in the name of ethics and history but in fact, according to modernism and, even more so, postmodernism, it distorts these ideas to promote ideology and elitism. The only way to combat this attack on the vulnerable tribe is to elevate it to a culture. "Each has its meaning to its inhabitants," writes Stimpson. Who would question this? But to announce it with such oracular understatement is to charge "meaning" with the metaphysical power reserved for culture in traditional humanist discourse; the members of a tribe "inhabit" their world, a region of the mind. If the "genteel tribalism" of Anglo-Saxon arrogance presumed to define the American scene in decades past, the explicit tribalism of today's anthropological "cultures" asserts itself with all the confidence of the new aesthetics of postmodernism, an aesthetics of tropological and intertextual indeterminacy: "These cultures interact, intersect, collide, influence each other. Our task is to understand these zones of interaction and to articulate national and international unities."

Stimpson's "unities" reach toward cosmopolitan awareness but much too warily to persuade us of her seriousness. And her closing demur on "pluralism" makes quite clear that she is far from willing to grant Jones's historical privileging of the "wisdom of the founding fathers," a specific moment in the history of ethical and cultural vision, with the final judgment on all those colliding "cultures" of our own time. In all fairness, one cannot entirely fault her skepticism. When we recall Jones's remarking the significance of the fact "that the word 'race' does not appear in the Declaration of Independence or the Constitution of the United States" and suggesting that this is added proof of the "universal humanity" inspiring Jefferson and company, we cannot help shaking a bit of deconstructed salt on Jones's linguistic insight and reflecting on the possibility that the absence of that particular word had more to do with guilty repression than brotherly love. The exclusion of Negro slaves from the social contract does not imply that the founding fathers were oblivious to "race" because they had translated themselves to an Enlightened state where the word no longer mattered.

Despite Jones's somewhat naive eagerness to inscribe the moment of the nation's birth with the epic vision of a morally heroic perception, there is, nevertheless, a historical insight in Jones's citing of the absence of "race" in the writings marking our cultural awakening, an insight that provides an explanation of black experience in America far more telling than the ruminations of tribal poets or the researches of anthropologists. It is simply this: as revolution and Romanticism continued on their parallel courses in the nineteenth century, the "human cry" of Anacreontic pleasure gradually took on the poignant and metaphysical authority of an absolute moral principle.

> The great, the unique contribution of romanticism to modernity is the insistence that every human being is a distinct and autonomous entity, whatever theories of education or of sociology or of political science or of evolution may say to the contrary. . . . There cannot be citizenship unless there is man, and the rights of man is a phrase essentially without meaning unless one believes, as the romantics did, that each human being is more than the totality of his own history.[24]

As the human identity of the black American became less and less deniable, first in the 1860s and then a hundred years later in the 1960s, he moved closer, in blood and crisis, to the rights guaranteed him by

24. HMJ, *Revolution and Romanticism*, 463–64.

our constitutional writings precisely because he was a "man" before he was anything else. When his humanity was finally recognized, the documents that omitted the mention of "race" became his personal documents. The "wisdom of the founding fathers" was even greater than they knew.

To trust in the significant historical moments of the past and to believe that they represent a kind of capital on which culture, at any moment in time, must draw to be itself is a proposition very much on the defensive at the present time in humanities departments of universities all over the nation. Multiculturalists are not saying that we should abandon the past, but they are insisting that we embrace the present with an ardor that makes many more traditionally centered academics very nervous indeed. As the debate becomes more rancorous, there is a tendency to stigmatize those opposing multiculturalism as the dominant curricular philosophy with accusations of racism, sexism, and other nasties. It is, unfortunately, reminiscent of McCarthyism; only this time liberals are being called reactionaries whereas in the 1950s they were called communists. Liberals, even when they are "strong" (in Harold Bloom's sense of "strong poets"), invite this kind of judgment because they are usually the true centrists, particularly in cultural matters. Political centrists often appear as if they are sitting on the fence; cultural centrists stand in the no man's land between the past and the present and point to the landscape of the future. Lionel Trilling was that kind of cultural liberal. And so was Howard Mumford Jones. What makes the cultural liberal appear far more conservative than he actually is? The answer lies in the cultural impatience of our time, its zeal to find in the present sufficient food for thought and spirit. This forces liberals, in order to combat the tyranny of the present, to turn to thinkers who dramatize the authority of the past.

Edmund Burke, whose career in politics and thought spanned a complex mixture of political liberalism and cultural conservatism, continues to speak for the cultural liberal in today's culture wars. At the same conference Catharine Stimpson attended, Gertrude Himmelfarb, the historian of nineteenth-century British politics and culture, participated in a discussion on "The Remaking of the Canon." Her use of Burke is instructive:

> Edmund Burke once explained why received opinion is an essential adjunct to reason: 'We are afraid to put men to live and trade each on

> his own private stock of reason; because we suspect that this stock in each man is small, and that the individuals would do better to avail themselves of the general bank and capital of nations, and of ages.'
>
> I think there is a lesson here for us today. It may explain why it is reasonable and proper to ask students, even scholars, to approach the past with an *a priori* respect, to give it, as Burke elsewhere said, 'the presumption of wisdom and virtue,' to accept, at least provisionally, until disproved by powerful evidence, the judgment of posterity about great writers and books. This calls for an initial suspension of private judgment in favor of authoritative opinion, the collective opinion of generations. And it is because we value that collective opinion, the 'capital of nations and ages,' that we are properly insecure about our judgments of contemporary literature—which is why, as Lionel Trilling brilliantly argued, contemporary literature should not be taught in schools and universities. It is also why the new edition of the Great Books, while adding (tentatively, as the editors tell us) some early twentieth-century books, stops short at midcentury, to give us time to think about the latest creations of our culture and to evaluate them, to see them in the larger perspective of the great books of the past.[25]

Nietzsche rejected both the notion that there are any laws in history and the notion that the Will to Power can afford to lodge its metaphysical entity in anything so vulnerable as a particular individual's consciousness, what he called the "superstition of subjectivity." Nevertheless, Nietzsche could not relinquish his stubborn ideality and in *The Use and Abuse of History* (1874) played with language in order to preserve what he called "monumental history" without legitimizing "history" itself: "The fundamental thought in our belief in humanity, which expresses itself in the demand for a *monumental* history, is that the great moments in the struggle of individuals form a chain, that in them a ridge of human peaks is linked through the millennia, and that for me the highest elements of such long-forgotten moments are still alive, clear and great."[26] The words themselves recall Jones's description of the greatest literary and cultural historians and remind us of his roots in the Renaissance valorization of epic as the preferred genre because of its ability to project models of ethical-heroic behavior. Hegel, as the reader will remember, dismissed epic as fantasy and therefore useless to the objective philosopher of history, who finds a more reliable model in the antithetical suffering of tragedy. Nietzsche agreed

25. "Changing Culture of the University," 364.
26. Julian Roberts, *German Philosophy: An Introduction*, 219, 227.

that "chaos" is the basic condition of human action, but, in contrast to Hegel, he did not think there were laws of history that could chart the suffering. On the contrary, the "chaos" is grist for heroic, monumental action; the Will to Power transcends all laws of causality but does answer to the ordering principle of ideality. Between Hegel, the rationalistic conservative, and Nietzsche, the eternal radical, stand Burke and his disciples—cultural liberals who reject determinisms of every stripe but are grateful for the objective reality of heroic thought and action in history.

Multiculturalists are anxious to preserve the uniqueness and rights of tribes and groups threatened by dominating entities and are therefore particularly sensitive to the ways that pluralism can force or seduce marginally situated cultures across their hyphens. This anxiety, which we saw in the words of Catharine Stimpson, reflects a legitimate concern of libertarians. America cannot escape the pressures of pluralism, but if we are to live up to our democratic principles we must protect the freedom of our many tribes to be themselves. Our variety is a changing phenomenon; no one knew this better than Jones. He was enthralled by the regional differences of our vast republic, but he was even more impressed at the ability of the historical American, born in the Age of Discovery and matured in the Age of Reason, to wrestle with the land and, despite a rich and various cultural memory, give it a new name. "It seems to me the humanist concerned for American studies . . . must begin by understanding that the United States is the first nation in history to be created on philosophical assumptions—assumptions that in fact boldly denied the premises of both Aristotle and Machiavelli."[27]

Jones's citing of these two philosophers cast out a wide net, but we know what he meant: that the United States is based on ideas that reject both the fate of nature and the fate of psychology as absolutely powerful determinants. The things that are binding to the American are his contractual ties to precisely those ideas that challenge Aristotle and Machiavelli, and Jones was explicit in locating these ideas in that moment of "monumental history" known as the Western Enlightenment, a moment identified with epic action and thought free of the need to defer to tragedy. Multiculturalism is guided, above all, by an

27. HMJ, *The Scholar as American*, 15.

emotion central to tragedy—compassion. Compassion belongs to the "human cry," but it is not all of it:

> Misunderstanding Hardy's famous statement that to arrive at the best demands a look at the worst, those who stress the wickedness of man, the debility of society, the vacuity of culture, and the propriety of violence, degeneracy, and failure as themes for art argue, to be sure, that the profound sympathy they wish to evoke for the human predicament is on the side of the angels. It is. But this is to substitute emotionalism for philosophy. . . . Man's inhumanity to man has made countless thousands mourn ever since Achilles mistreated the body of Hector, but to stop with this commonplace is to beg the central issue. Let us not mistake compassion, which is part of wisdom, for the whole of wisdom, which is the goal, at least, of the humanities.[28]

Today "compassion" has brought us to "political correctness," and there are many, among both majority and minority groups, who doubt the "wisdom" of our situation. Although Jones insisted that "young Americanists" must "know the European culture from which we spring," he was, as I have already noted, one of the first to assert the importance of bringing African American writers, women writers, Asian philosophy, and, perhaps most emphatically, Latin American culture to the attention of all those presuming truly to understand American culture itself. Archibald MacLeish had called Jones's attention to the rich intellectual traditions of Mexico; true to his belief that a culture wise enough to maintain and address the best achievements of its own past was a culture in touch with the humanist imperative, Jones began to argue that without a richer understanding of Latin American culture we in the North risked becoming crucially ignorant of just how "America" had evolved from its European or Atlantic origins. In other words, for a humanist to study the cultures of South America did not primarily constitute the discovery of an exotic "other," or what contemporary theorists might see as a multicultural confrontation somewhat similar to what happens in intertextuality. No, what excited Jones was the historical fact that Latin America was closer culturally to the Renaissance and North America to the Enlightenment and that together the two cultures provided a historical paradigm for the "monumental" eruptions of European experience that had spilled across the Atlantic and were still carving out the culture

28. Ibid., 17.

that everyone calls "American" but that most do not yet fully understand in its obscure but pervasive unity.

Jones admired Alfonso Reyes, "the last universal literary man," a prototype, according to MacLeish, for "a return to the concept of the man of letters in the modern world." All of that sounds wistful in the last decades of the twentieth century, when the "man of letters" has yielded the field to the "literary theorist" and the "modern world" has turned "postmodern." The notion that any literary sensibility can presume to universality is, as I have demonstrated, a position kept rather quietly by those whose pieties make it impossible for them to relinquish it. As an ideal, this Platonic dream is certainly a European creation, but European despair after World War I directed intellectual energies to its dismantling, a skeptical job that continued unabated through the aftermath of World War II and reached its peak in the linguistic skepticism and cultural relativism following the "bonfires" of 1968. I have suggested that the language of postmodernist tropological criticism is in harmony with the particularist dogma of multiculturalism. The figure of speech is like the tribal group, a mysteriously irreducible atom that cannot, must not yield to a superseding entity; furthermore, since each is the foundation of what presumes to absorb it—language in the case of metaphor and humane culture in the case of the tribe—it is useless to Platonize because metaphor and tribe will deconstruct whatever presumes to transcend their immanence. The chair of the English department at Wesleyan University, Khachig Tololyan, has recently observed that his university's attempt to honor the agenda of "compassion" has led to making "multiculturalism . . . a mechanism for multiplying differences." What Professor Tololyan tells us about the lengths to which multiculturalism at Wesleyan seems willing to go sounds very much in tune with Derridean indeterminacy: "For example . . . in multicultural discussions here, someone says: 'Yes, but don't lesbians of that group have separate problems? Aren't they different? Don't lesbians of that group who are working class have even more separate problems?'"[29]

In 1939, just before the beginning of the greatest war of the century, Alfonso Reyes wrote a short essay, "Thoughts on the American Mind." Here is a representative passage:

29. Ibid., 11; "Interview of Khachig Tololyan," *Los Angeles Times,* January 4, 1992, A17.

> For this beautiful harmony which I envisage, the American mind is peculiarly suited, for our mentality, at the same time that it is deeply rooted in our soil, is, as I have said, by nature international. The explanation of this lies not merely in the fact that America is fitted to be the crucible of that "cosmic race" of the future which Vasconcelos has dreamed of, but also in the fact that we have had to go to the great centers of Europe for our cultural equipment, and in this way have become accustomed to handle ideas of foreign origin as though they were our own. While the European has never had to approach America to construct the system of his world, the American studies, knows, follows Europe from the time he starts to school. . . . Our innate internationalism, based, fortunately, on the historic brotherhood that links our numerous republics together, gives the American mind an indisputably peace-loving inclination. With an even more skillful hand this intervenes and overrules the threat of armed conflict, and in the international field it makes itself felt among those groups which are more contaminated by the political pugnaciousness now in fashion. This will facilitate a gracious junction with the pacifistic idealism of the greatest North American minds.
>
> Our America should live as though it were always making ready to realize the dream to which its discovery gave rise among the thinkers of Europe: the dream of Utopia, of the happy republic, which lent peculiar warmth to the pages of Montaigne as he reflected on the surprises and marvels of the New World.[30]

If the idealism, utopianism, and internationalism of the above passage inspired Howard Mumford Jones to the research and meditation that finally bore fruit in his Pulitzer Prize–winning book, *O Strange New World: American Culture, the Formative Years* (1964), those same ideas will strike contemporary readers as historically naive. Have not the intervening fifty years simply continued the same kind of ugly and often brutal interventions by the United States in the internal affairs of Latin America that had prevailed in the nineteenth century? Have not the Latin American nations themselves been torn by civil strife, economic injustice, and anarchy? The truth is that despite the apparently endless cycle of intervention and internecine strife, the nations of the Americas have in the twentieth century, by and large, avoided international war; they have been spared the global conflicts of Europe and Asia. Indeed, there has been a tacit understanding quite apart from the Monroe Doctrine that not only would Europe stay out of the Americas but that North America

30. In *The Position of America and Other Essays,* 38–39.

would shoulder the responsibility of involvement in European and Asian wars in order to protect all American nations. There is something that protects the American world from confusing its cultural and ethnic differences with the philosophical and historical ideas that gave it birth. Ironically, just as Reyes says and as Jones demonstrates in his extensive cultural histories, our differences are subsumed by our European cultural heritage. Our cultural past prevents us from totalizing our tribal present. We are still committed to Whitman's "Passage to India"—what Reyes calls the "dream of Utopia"—and the people of our two hemispheres continue to revel in their regional uniqueness as they pursue the "happiness" promised them by Montaigne and Montesquieu, More and Locke, Cervantes and Rousseau.

There is in this search of a home for the mind and heart that will transcend the tribal home a strong epic dimension. The epic quester traditionally calls on tribes but rarely lingers; he may make his own tribe in the image of a vision, or he may choose to leave the tribe behind. Odysseus and Jacob, Huckleberry Finn and Don Quixote share all of the above in a variety of paradigms. Odysseus, the archetypal epic hero, finally returns to his tribe, but apocryphal versions of his ultimate fate surface in Dante and Tennyson to remind us that his real destination lies altogether beyond tribalism. The good fortune of American culture is that it is rooted historically in dreams that rose from ideas emanating from the cosmopolitan watersheds of European history. Never was Europe less tribal than during the Renaissance and the Enlightenment. Germany's awakening is compounded of Enlightenment and Romanticism; the Enlightenment was, as Hegel argued, "belated," and as compensation for being the last in line to partake of the elevation connected with the dual heritage of Renaissance and Enlightenment, Germany felt the need to elevate its Romantic genius. This was done, as Jones recognized, by establishing the metaphysical authority of subjectivity. There was a cost, however. With subjectivity as the primal truth, the external world was either internalized or diminished. In any case, the immediate environment of the self became its castle. For millions of ordinary Germans, this idea was understood as *Heimat*—the tribal home posing as culture. In today's Germany, argues Jane Kramer, "Heimat . . . is a code for German fundamentalism; it takes the landscape for its text, a catalogue of simple, selfish 'rural' values for its theme, and 'being German again' for its intention."[31] Since Kramer made this observation, Germany is once again united and this time in the image of its democratized western half, a region identified politically for the last fifty years with the United States. So far, the traditions of *Heimat* seem to be playing a greater role in the former "East" than the more recently acquired values of democracy and cosmopolitanism in the former "West." If *Heimat* becomes the glue to hold the new Germany together, then it will once again become a tribal nation. The landscape of *Heimat* is not the epic landscape of Jones's vision of democratic energy. We cannot forget that fascism not only glorified the community over the individual, as noted earlier, but also excluded the marginal or cosmopolitan person in order to maintain the trope of *Heimat* as a cultural ideal—to establish a political unity without culture.

Multiculturalism, which believes itself diametrically opposed to the intolerance and totalitarian values of an ideology like fascism, must consider very carefully its intellectual options when attacking history. Social and political history is indeed a litany of sins: colonialism, imperialism, sexism, and racism head the list in the best of the Western democracies—and the list is much longer. Cultural history, on the other hand, provides us with the tools we need to fix the leaks in social and political systems. Cultural history has, of course, its own sins—dogmatic religion, superstitious science, and corrupt scholarship, to name only a few—but at the same time the thinking that goes on in culture is the only way the ideologies of politics can be reshaped by ideas. To conflate social and political reality with culture, to argue that they are the same, is to ignore what makes the humanities unique, as Jones has told us. It forces us to accuse the past, in a categorical way, of being responsible for the ills of the present and thereby cuts us off from whatever the past might provide to help us correct those ills. Unfortunately, multiculturalist spokesmen tend to insist that whatever is produced by contemporary ethnic, women, or gay writers has cultural significance because it is politically or socially challenging; such views valorize ideology at the expense of ideas.

We know, of course, that the conviction that culture could be free of ideology, that it could stand in critical relation towards it, is considered by postmodern intellectuals as a nostalgic illusion. They have read their Nietzsche, and he has made it absolutely clear that what we

31. *Europeans*, 494.

call a "truth," our philosophical and aesthetic heritage, in other words, the "humanities," is nothing but dead language:

> What, then, is truth? A mobile army of metaphors, metonyms, and anthropomorphisms—in short, a sum of human relations, which have been enhanced, transposed, and embellished poetically and rhetorically, and which after long use seem firm, canonical, and obligatory to a people: truths are illusions about which one has forgotten that this is what they are; metaphors which are worn out. . . . We still do not know where the truth comes from; for as yet we have heard only of the obligation imposed by society that it should exist: to be truthful means using the customary metaphors—in moral terms: the obligation to lie according to a fixed convention, to lie herd-like in a style obligatory to all.

Nietzsche's words resonate in the thought of Hayden White, Frederic Jameson, Barbara Johnson, and others I have juxtaposed in these pages to Howard Mumford Jones. Postmodernism has taken Nietzsche's reduction of the "sum of human relations" to its tropological level as an a priori principle for all further thought and writing in the humanities. Certainly what we have seen of the history of the typological mode in historical humanism precludes so sweeping a dismissal of all that humanism has accomplished. Reducing the typological to the tropological establishes an analytical frame of reference that automatically diminishes whatever is analyzed. The wonder of literature is not in its being a field of infinite linguistic combinations but rather that in spite of this condition literature continually provides us with unities that transcend the undermining and contradictory pressure of its primary parts. And if this is true of literature, it is also true of society at its most human. The "sum of human relations" is not, as Nietzsche himself implied in *The Use and Abuse of History,* merely a tally of rhetorical figures. Indeed, the shining examples of "monumental history" are "for all their multiplicity typically the same, and as the universal presence of unalterable types they are a static formation of unchanged value and eternally identical significance."[32]

Jones made a typological pact with history that enabled him to chart an epic course. Postmodernism's tropological pact with history derives dignity from its Hegelian connections with tragedy, but the heart of postmodernism is not with Hegel but his arch critic, Nietzsche—in

32. Friedrich Nietzsche, "On Truth and Lie in an Extra Moral Sense," in *Thus Spoke Zarathustra,* in *The Portable Nietzsche,* 47–48; Roberts, *German Philosophy,* 228.

any case the Nietzsche who refused to recognize the dialectical thrust of history and rationalized his ideas of "monumental history" by calling them "unhistorical." Perhaps Nietzsche protested too much, or perhaps he was merely indulging his gift for playful contradiction, the legacy of Romantic irony theorized by Friedrich Schlegel and implemented brilliantly by Heinrich Heine. The Romantic ironist explodes his own creations and derives inspiration from undermining the illusions he mounts. The reader will remember that Jones translated Heine and admired as well as identified with his ironic masks. Jones's Anacreontic typology owes a great deal to Heine's messianic-comic classicism:

> I wish to destroy the new temple
> And fight for you, you ancient gods,
> For you and your ambrosial law
> ("The Gods of Greece")

In Heine's *The Exile of the Gods* Christ is Hellenized and becomes "the savior of the senses" and the "divine liberator." It was E. M. Butler who summed up the connection of all this to Nietzsche: "Dionysus, who came late into Greece, came late into Germany. Heine ushered him in and then left it to Friedrich Nietzsche to see that he got his rights."[33]

Nietzsche's case for Dionysus was so brilliantly argued that now, at the end of the twentieth century, we can safely suggest that perhaps Dionysus got more than his rights. Heine asked that his gravestone recall that he had been a "a soldier in the struggle for the liberation of humanity." Nietzsche's Dionysian "Overman" doubted the wisdom of liberating *all* of humanity: "That everyone may learn to read, in the long run corrupts not only writing but also thinking. Once the spirit was God, then he became man, and now he even becomes rabble." Nietzsche's elitism rises directly from his disgust at the abuse of language in history, and that disgust is, I believe, the repressed belief at the heart of postmodernism's revolt against all typologies of unity or transcendence. What is missing in postmodernist theories, despite the reputation of Derridean wit, is the levity, the "gay science," that Nietzsche so admired in Heine and that Nietzsche himself never completely lost. Howard Mumford Jones was fond of citing the following

33. *The Tyranny of Greece over Germany,* 300.

well-known lines from *Thus Spake Zarathustra,* part 1, section 5: "I say unto you: one must still have chaos in oneself to be able to give birth to a dancing star."[34] The "chaos" is inseparable from "subjectivity," and we have seen how Jones learned to respect its demands. But chaos can have a purpose other than merely its own exercise.

Walter Benjamin's solution to the irreparable break with tradition (*Traditionsbruch*) and loss of spiritual and intellectual authority (*Autoritätsverlust*) was to sift through the resulting chaos for the commanding fragment or detail that might reveal something of the wholeness of which it was originally an integral part. Benjamin thought these shards were allegorical: "Allegories stand in relation to thought as ruins to things" (*Allegorien sind in Reiche des Gedankens, was Ruinen in Reiche der Dinge*). Postmodernism has appropriated Benjamin's ruminations on allegory, among the oldest of tropes, to wage war on what it sees as totalizing symbolizations, past or present: "Only with allegory do distancing, dehumanization, rupture, fragmentation come to full expression" (*Nur in der Allegorie lassen sich Entfremdung, Verdinglichung, Bruch, Zerstückelung ausdrucken*).[35] Jones's wavering between the "encyclopedic" and the "selective" was his own devil-may-care way of engaging chaos without forsaking wholeness (*Ganzheit*) and is, therefore, closer in spirit to Benjamin than are many of his postmodernist disciples. Both Jones and Benjamin were unsystematic, spent the bulk of their creativity in commentary on the works of others, collected data (Jones, facts; Benjamin, citations—and books), and sought in literary and historical research explanations of the heritage that lay about either in the "ruins" of the past or the materializations of the present. Benjamin's strange blend of Marxism and messianic speculation is similar to Jones's unwavering trust in the dialogue between popular and traditional culture. Jones, on his polymathic trek, was as robust as Benjamin's *Flâneur*—the Baudelairean wanderer in the "passages" of Paris—was pale and withdrawn. Jones would have recognized him as the latest version of the "Anonymous Young Man" and, I think, would nevertheless have admitted to a strange affinity. If Ben-

34. Nietzsche, "Zarathustra's Speeches, On Reading and Writing" and "Zarathustra's Prologue 5," in *The Portable Nietzsche,* 152, 129.

35. Walter Benjamin, *Ursprung des Deutschen Trauerspiels* (Origins of the German tragic drama), 155; Gabriele Dietrich, "Jüdische-Prophetisches in der modernen deutschen Philosophie und Soziologie" (Prophetic Judaism in modern German philosophy and sociology), 380.

jamin's "ruins" seemed to reveal the outlines of mysterious unities, Jones's wide and often dissonant learning occasionally empowered brilliant synthesis.

* * *

In early 1992, the Before Columbus Foundation published anthologies of fiction and poetry written by winners of the Foundation's annual American Book Award, which was established in 1980. These writers speak for a wide range of social, ethnic, racial, and gender groups. "Since 1976," says the back cover of the fiction volume, "the . . . Foundation has been devoted to the task of redefining our notion of mainstream American literature to reflect this country's multicultural, multiethnic, and multiracial diversity." In 1990, Ishmael Reed, poet and cofounder of the Foundation, said in a speech in Seattle, "Our vision of the future has room for the Asian, the African, as well as the Western (European). We don't see these as dangerous times, as do the paranoid monoculturalists."[36] Reed's attempt to bracket our Western heritage ("European") seems curiously defensive. After all, by late twentieth century, Western "culture" has already absorbed the creative energies of non-European minds in record numbers. Much of post-colonial literature, for example, is no more European than it is Caribbean or Indian. Derek Walcott has written eloquently of his love for the English language, which saved him from drowning in silence; the language of his beloved St. Lucia islanders is not a written one (*The Arkansas Testament*, 1987). V. S. Naipaul has fused Arnoldian values with a marginal sensibility bridging the West Indies, India, and Oxford (for example, *The Enigma of Arrival*, 1987). Both of these writers, poet and novelist, have redefined the emotions of homelessness and sanctuary; they have enlarged the old mystique of Eliot and Auden's "alienation" so that it now resonates with elegiac, epic, and tragic chords as reminiscent of Homer, Sophocles, and Euripides as anything the Anglo-Saxon moderns themselves managed to sound. There is not and never has been a "monoculture" worthy of the name. Finally, Africans and Asians in the United States are making

36. Gundars Strads, Kathryn Trueblood, and Shawn Wong, "Introduction: Redefining the Mainstream," in Ishmael Reed, Kathryn Trueblood, and Shawn Wong, eds., *The Before Columbus Foundation Fiction Anthology: Selections from the American Book Awards, 1980–1990*, xi.

and will continue to make "cultural" statements in direct proportion to their immersion in what, in the fullest sense, is going on around them—past and present.

Ishmael Reed ends his second essay in the *Before Columbus Foundation Fiction Anthology* with a portentous sentence: "American literature is an ocean."[37] The trope of "mainstream" yielding to the trope of "ocean" suggests a mighty river flowing into uncharted seas. This trope changes our grasp of America from a "strange new world" to a measureless space of unfathomable depth; from the richly inviting landscapes of Cooper and Jefferson to a monotonous infinity; from the heroic and epic possibilities of Fitzgerald's Dutch sailors as they row eagerly toward the shore in the lyrical period closing *The Great Gatsby*—"borne back ceaselessly into the past"—to an amorphous liquidity of insoluble difference. Beyond a doubt many of the stories in this anthology are powerful accounts of experience once seen as marginal to conventional American social and political reality. But culturally they are as rooted in the literary traditions of realism, naturalism, surrealism, and various forms of psychological symbolism as any other fiction in the modern world. These genres blend, as they have for generations, but their cultural vitality will be determined by time, learned judgment, and the common reader—not by their ethnic, gender, or racial origin. Ibsen is the father of dramatic realism, not Norwegian dramatic realism. The Jew, Heine, and the man of Slavic background, Nietzsche, revolutionized German literature. The most powerfully imagined male character in nineteenth-century British fiction is the achievement of a woman writer: Emily Brontë's Heathcliff. It is also true that nowhere in the novels of a dozen accomplished nineteenth-century women writers can one find a single literary creation comparable to Flaubert's Emma or Tolstoy's Natasha and Anna. Conrad, the Pole, is probably the greatest late Victorian novelist. Joyce, the Irishman, is universally considered the greatest modern novelist in the English language. Picasso, the Spaniard, is the greatest modern painter of his adopted country, France. Bellow, the American Jew, has written one of the best American Protestant novels of the mid-twentieth century, *Henderson the Rain King*. This novel also includes one of the most heroic portraits of a black male in modern American literature, King Dahfu.

37. Ishmael Reed, "The Ocean of American Literature," in Reed, Trueblood, and Wong, eds., *Before Columbus Foundation Fiction Anthology*, xxvii.

The cultural world has tended not to be ethnocentric since the Enlightenment. A deep appreciation for the tribal underlies all important art created since the late eighteenth century, but that appreciation is usually the first rung of a ladder reaching both deeper and higher than tribal identity. Without a profound identification with our tribal origins, we risk shallowness and deracination; indeed, it is no exaggeration to argue, as did young Goethe's mentor, Johann Gottfried Herder, that to deny our tribe is to invalidate our candidacy for culture. Fearful assimilation into a mainstream group is nothing but self-hate, and it is never the path to cosmopolitanism; the alienated artist is almost a contradiction in terms. Nevertheless, the tribal cannot be an end in itself for the artist, or he risks the fate of having to lose his humanity in order to remain faithful to his tribe. When tribalism ceases to be an avenue toward humanity, the artist must often reject his tribe in order to preserve its best self in his own art. "In the works which I take with me is my home," wrote Thomas Mann in exile. "They are language, German language and thought, the individually developed traditional treasures of my country and people. Where I am, is Germany."[38] The tribal heritage must be "individually developed." Merely to trade on our ethnicity, color, or sex in order to claim individuality is to betray the sacrifices of all those geniuses of every ethnicity, color, or sex whose victories in philosophy, science, art, and moral courage have provided us with models for being that persuade us we are human before we are anything else.

Howard Mumford Jones understood the ethnic principle, the rich native soil from which culture springs. He would have applauded the openness of the Before Columbus Foundation anthologies and their commitment to egalitarianism. But he would have demurred at their eagerness to insist that their political and social tolerance was a sufficient standard for cultural validation in the literary arts. He knew from his wide learning what an important role the past plays in guiding our sense of cultural value.

> Profound changes . . . go forward rapidly in the social and economic spheres whereas the arts remain cautious, conservative, and European. The praise of authors, painters, dramatists, sculptors, and architects here is long that they are no worse than Europe, sometimes as good,

38. In Anthony Heilbut, *Exiled in Paradise: German Refugee Artists and Intellectuals in America from the 1930s to the Present*, 306.

> and occasionally better. We note how the recognition of Whitman comes late, and how we have to wait until the twentieth century for a Frank Lloyd Wright and how, after a thousand tries, we do not produce a dramatist of power until Eugene O'Neill.

Jones's historical sense told him that culture has to brew. There is appeal in the Before Columbus Foundation's belief that "the ingredients of America's 'melting pot' are not only distinct, but integral to the unique constitution of American culture—the whole comprises the parts. There are no outsiders."[39] And there should be none. But once they are recognized, all the tribes must answer to an epic roll call that goes beyond enumeration. The whole is greater than its parts. What is cooking in the pot, if we are to serve it at some great Alexandrian Wedding at Susa of the future (where, this time, brides and grooms will choose one another freely), must be greater than the sum of its tropes.

39. HMJ, *The Scholar as American*, 13; Strads, Trueblood, and Wong, "Introduction," in Reed, Trueblood, and Wong, eds., *Before Columbus Foundation Fiction Anthology*, xii.

Appendix

HOWARD MUMFORD JONES, 1892–1980

The following memoir was originally prepared at Harvard for the "Faculty Minutes" by a committee after Jones's death in 1980. The committee included Daniel Aaron, Herschel Baker, Douglas W. Bryant, and John P. Dawson and was chaired by Jerome H. Buckley. This memoir and thirty others of former English professors at Harvard was recently published in *Harvard Scholars in English, 1890–1990,* edited by Walter Jackson Bate, Michael Shinagel, and James Engell (Cambridge: Harvard University Press, 1991).

Howard Mumford Jones, historian of American culture, man of letters, and one of the most distinguished humanists of our time, died in Cambridge on May 11, 1980, at the age of eighty-eight. Early in his long career he established himself as a major literary and social historian with a fresh and vital approach to his field of inquiry. His *America and French Culture* (1927) placed a new emphasis on the Continental European sources of our national heritage at a time when most Americanists were too exclusively preoccupied with the New England component and its Puritan derivations. Over the next twenty years he wrote a number of substantial essays and monographs on many writers and intellectual movements from the colonial period through the early twentieth century and on the general theory of American literature. His principal American studies, however, appeared much later. Well after his retirement, which he grudgingly accepted at seventy, he published his magisterial trilogy: *O Strange New World* (1964), *The Age of Energy* (1971), and *Revolution and Romanticism* (1974). Though the title of the second of these describes the five expansive decades following the Civil War, it appropriately characterized the man himself, for Howard Jones's intellectual energy was prodigious and perpetual. At the time of his death, having completed his *Autobiography,* his eleventh book since retirement, he was at work on yet another spacious cultural history, to be called *The Old West: an Unconventional View,* one of the most vigorous chapters of which presents the American cowboy, a figure he could appraise with particular zest and sympathy.

Howard Jones was the least parochial of American scholars, prepared, as he always was, to place his subject, whether it was a single American author or the whole United States, in the broadest, most cosmopolitan perspective. And his expertise ranged far beyond our national boundaries or the narrowed concentration of any single discipline. He had an impressive command of British intellectual history and a contagious enthusiasm for the Victorian novel. He wrote a good deal of original verse, both lyrical and satiric, and clever parodies of his favorite poets. As a young man he skillfully translated Heine's *Nordsee* and a group of medieval songs, and later he made a memorable version of the solemn *Dies Irae* of Thomas of Celano. He prepared bibliographies and study guides, edited a volume of eighteenth-century plays, and with his wife, Bessie Zaban Jones, assembled a spirited anthology, *The Many Voices of Boston* (1975). His *Treasury of Scientific Prose* (1965), compiled with I. Bernard Cohen, suggests his keen interest in "natural philosophy" and his high regard for the masters of technical exposition. And the book he liked best among his own, *The Harp That Once* (1937), a biography of Thomas Moore, reflects his wide knowledge not only of Anglo-Irish literature but also of the larger European romantic movement. Perhaps most insistently of all, his many shorter works, collections of essays and public lectures, testify to his tremendous vigor and eloquence as defender of the humanities, an intellectual drive that persisted to the last. It was the comprehensive vision of the humanist, perpetually alert to the interdependency of our world, that prompted a letter less than two weeks before his death to the editor of the *Journal of the History of Ideas,* declaring the need for a deeper understanding of Chinese ideology and of the ethical assumptions of modern India.

Like Hamlin Garland, whom he served in high-school days as a secretary-typist, Howard Jones was proudly a "son of the middle border." Born in Saginaw, Michigan, on April 16, 1892, he spent his youth in La Crosse, Wisconsin, where he attended Normal School before going on for his B.A. at the University in Madison. He received his M.A. from Chicago in 1915, but then stubbornly refused to take courses, required for the Chicago doctorate, which he himself had already taught at that institution. Fifteen honorary degrees in later years indicate that the lack of a Ph.D. proved no considerable handicap in a teaching career that carried him from Texas to Montana to North Carolina and in 1930 to the University of Michigan.

In 1936, precisely the middle year of his long life, he came to Harvard as one of the principal Tercentenary speakers and here remained as Professor of English. Though he quickly acquired a remarkable understanding of New England modes and manners, his roots were distinctly Western, or at least Middle Western, in the world beyond the Alleghenies. If Harvard at the time was largely Eastern, exclusive, and self-contained, Howard Jones helped open it—not without some resistance—to a wider American context. His energy, verve, and mercurial temper, at first disconcerting to some of his more restrained colleagues, endeared him to countless students, who found him both generous and exacting. His intellectual demand on scholarship as on literature was indeed strenuous. Of a writer he mostly admired, he wrote: "Faulkner gave man a soul capable of compassion, sacrifice and endurance, but Faulkner left out intelligence. Future novelists may yet return to accepting intelligence as essential in human nature and add to the democracy of the heart the democracy of the mind." To all those who worked closely with him Howard Jones's erudition was often intimidating. Yet his kindness of heart was as pervasive as his intellectual rigor. Over the years he contributed much of his own double democracy to Harvard, which, in turn, meant much to him: "If intellectual freedom," he once declared, "has her home anywhere, it is in the Harvard Yard." Within that privileged space, his study, Widener 115, became for many of his students a center and a symbol of the free intelligence. From such a vantage he himself ranged the University collections as few others have ever done until he had developed the special intimacy with the Library, its holdings and organization, that is reflected in his late work as editor of the *Harvard Library Bulletin.*

In 1960 Howard Jones was appointed the first Abbott Lawrence Lowell Professor of the Humanities. The next year, receiving another sort of chair, the armchair presented to staff members after twenty-five years of service, he remarked with characteristic wit: "Harvard is, so far as I know, the only institution in the country that says to employees of long standing, 'I think you had better sit down.'" But he himself was scarcely willing to sit for long. Though he wrote and published much after his retirement in 1962, he eagerly accepted visiting professorships at the Universities of Wisconsin and Jerusalem and at Middlebury College, and he continued his lifelong practice of giving lectures and addresses at assemblies and convocations all across the country from Maine to California.

Howard Jones attained widespread recognition for his scholarship and public service. He was three times a Guggenheim Fellow. He was awarded the Jusserand Medal of the American Historical Association in 1934, the Pulitzer and Emerson Prizes in 1964, and the Phi Beta Kappa Medal and Prize in 1973. He served for one year (1943–1944) as Dean of the Harvard Graduate School of Arts and Sciences, for two years (1959–1961) as Chairman of the Weil Institute for Studies in Religion and the Humanities, for two terms as a member of the Council of the American Philosophical Society, and from 1944 to 1951 as President of the American Academy of Arts and Sciences. He did much to revitalize the American Council of Learned Societies as its Chairman (1955–1959), and he worked for a complete reorganization of the Modern Language Association as its President in 1965.

Howard Mumford Jones is survived by his wife, Bessie Zaban Jones, a daughter by a first marriage, Eleanor Jones Ingersoll, two grandchildren, and one great grandchild.

Bibliography

Works by Howard Mumford Jones

The Age of Energy: Varieties of American Experience, 1865–1915. New York: Viking, 1971.

America and French Culture, 1750–1848. Chapel Hill: University of North Carolina Press, 1927.

American Humanism: Its Meaning for World Survival. New York: Harper, 1957.

"American Scholarship and American Literature." *American Literature* 8 (May 1936): 115–24.

"American Studies in Higher Education." In *Essays on American Literature in Honor of Jay B. Hubbell,* edited by Clarence Ghodes. Durham: Duke University Press, 1967.

Belief and Disbelief in American Literature. Chicago: University of Chicago Press, 1967.

"Be Obscure, Clearly." *Buffalo Evening News,* June 24, 1965.

The Bright Medusa. Urbana: University of Illinois Press, 1952.

Education and World Tragedy. Cambridge: Harvard University Press, 1946.

"The European Background." In *Literary History of the United States,* edited by Robert E. Spiller, Willard Thorpe, Thomas H. Johnson, Henry Seidel Canby, and Richard M. Ludwig. New York: Macmillan, 1963.

The Frontier in American Fiction: Four Lectures on the Relation of Landscape to Literature. Jerusalem: Hebrew University Press, 1956.

The Harp That Once: A Chronicle of the Life of Thomas Moore. New York: Holt, 1937.

Heine's Poem: The North Sea. Introduced and translated by Howard Mumford Jones. Chicago: Open Court Publishing Co., 1916.

History and the Contemporary: Essays in Nineteenth-Century Literature. Madison: University of Wisconsin Press, 1964.

Howard Mumford Jones: An Autobiography. Madison: University of Wisconsin Press, 1979.

"Humanism Today." *Harvard Library Bulletin* 23 (October 1975): 365–78.

Ideas in America. Cambridge: Harvard University Press, 1944.

"The Influence of European Ideas in Nineteenth-Century America." *American Literature* 7 (November 1935): 241–73.

"Introduction." In *Primer of Intellectual Freedom,* edited by Howard Mumford Jones, ix–xv. Cambridge: Harvard University Press, 1949.

Jeffersonianism and the American Novel. New York: Columbia University Teachers College Press, 1966.

The King in Hamlet. Austin: University of Texas Press, 1918.

The Life of Moses Coit Tyler. Ann Arbor: University of Michigan Press, 1933.

One Great Society: Humane Learning in the United States. New York: Harcourt, Brace & Co., 1959.

O Strange New World. American Culture: The Formative Years. New York: Viking, 1964.

The Pursuit of Happiness. Cambridge: Harvard University Press, 1952.

"The Pygmy and the Giant." *PMLA* 81 (March 1966): 8–11.

Review of *On Native Grounds,* by Alfred Kazin. *Saturday Review of Literature* 25 (October 31, 1942): 5–6.

Revolution and Romanticism. Cambridge: The Belknap Press of Harvard University Press, 1974.

The Scholar as American. Abbot Lawrence Lowell Inaugural Lecture. Cambridge: Harvard University Press, 1960.

Scholarship, Novelty, and Teaching: An Address in Memory of the Late William Charvat. Columbus: Ohio State University Press, 1968.

The Theory of American Literature. Ithaca: Cornell University Press, 1948; reissued 1965.

A Treasury of Scientific Prose: A Nineteenth-Century Anthology. Edited by Howard Mumford Jones and I. Bernard Cohen. Boston: Little, Brown & Co., 1963.

Violence and Reason: A Book of Essays. New York: Atheneum, 1969.

Secondary Sources

Abrams, M. H. *Doing Things with Texts: Essays in Criticism and Critical Theory.* Edited by Michael Fischer. New York: Norton, 1989.

———. *Glossary of Literary Terms.* 5th ed. New York: Holt, Rinehart and Winston, 1988.

Adams, Henry. *The Education of Henry Adams: An Autobiography*. Boston: Houghton Mifflin, 1918.

———. *The Letters of Henry Adams, 1892–1918*. Edited by Worthington Chauncey Ford. Boston: Houghton Mifflin, 1938.

Alter, Robert. "Review of Revolution and Romanticism." *New York Times*, September 8, 1974.

Arac, Jonathan. *Critical Genealogies: Historical Situations for Postmodern Literary Studies*. New York: Columbia University Press, 1989.

Babbitt, Irving. *Literature and the American College: Essays in the Defense of the Humanities*. Boston: Houghton Mifflin, 1908.

Barthes, Roland. *Critical Essays*. Translated by Richard Howard. Evanston: Northwestern University Press, 1972.

———. *Image-Music-Text*. Translated by Stephen Heath. Glasgow: William Collins, 1977.

Bate, Walter Jackson. *Samuel Johnson*. New York: Harcourt Brace Jovanovich, 1977.

Bate, Walter Jackson, ed. *Criticism: The Major Texts*. New York: Harcourt Brace Jovanovich, 1970.

Bate, Walter Jackson, Michael Shinagel, and James Engell, eds. *Harvard Scholars in English, 1890–1990*. Cambridge: Harvard University Press, 1991.

Baudelaire, Charles. *The Mirror of Art: Critical Studies*. Translated and edited by Jonathan Mayne. New York: Doubleday, 1956.

Benjamin, Walter. *Ursprung des Deutschen Trauerspiels*. Edited by Rolf Tiedemann. Frankfurt am Main: Suhrkamp Verlag, 1978.

Blackmur, R. P. *Henry Adams*. Edited by Veronica A. Makowsky. Foreword by Denis Donoghue. New York: Harcourt Brace Jovanovich, 1980.

Bloom, Harold. *Ruin the Sacred Truths: Poetry and Belief from the Bible to the Present*. Cambridge: Harvard University Press, 1989.

Blumenthal, Henry. *American and French Culture, 1800–1900: Interchanges in Art, Science, Literature, and Society*. Baton Rouge: Louisiana State University Press, 1975.

Bové, Paul A. *Intellectuals in Power: A Genealogy of Critical Humanism*. New York: Columbia University Press, 1986.

Boyle, Nicholas. *The Poetry of Desire (1749–1790)*. Vol. 1 of *Goethe: The Poet and the Age*. Oxford: Clarendon Press, 1991.

Bridgman, Richard. "The American Studies of Henry Nash Smith." *American Scholar* 56 (Spring 1987): 259–68.

Brooks, Cleanth, and Robert Penn Warren. *Understanding Poetry: An Anthology for College Students*. New York: Holt, 1938.

Brooks, Van Wyck. *From a Writer's Notebook.* New York: E. P. Dutton, 1958.

Burke, Kenneth. *A Grammar of Motives: The Problems of Meaning in Dramatic Perspective.* New York: Prentice Hall, 1952.

Burnshaw, Stanley. *Robert Frost Himself.* New York: George Braziller, 1986.

Bush, Douglas. *Mythology and the Renaissance Tradition in English Poetry.* New York: Norton, 1963.

———. *Mythology and the Romantic Tradition in English Poetry.* New York: Norton, 1937.

Butler, E. M. *The Tyranny of Greece over Germany.* Boston: Beacon Press, 1958.

Carter, Everett. *The American Idea.* Chapel Hill: University of North Carolina Press, 1977.

Casebier, Allan. *Film and Phenomenology: Toward a Realist Theory of Cinematic Representation.* New York: Cambridge University Press, 1991.

Chase, Richard. *The Dramatic Vista: A Dialogue on Life and Letters in Contemporary America.* New York: Doubleday, 1958.

Clark, Robert. "The Absent Landscape of America's Eighteenth Century." In *Views of American Landscapes,* edited by M. Gridley and R. Lawson-Peebles, 81–89. Cambridge: Cambridge University Press, 1989.

Cohen, Ralph. "Do Postmodern Genres Exist?" In *Postmodern Genres,* edited by Marjorie Perloff. Norman: Oklahoma University Press, 1991.

Conant, James Bryant. *Education in a Divided World: The Function of the Public Schools in Our Unique Society.* Cambridge: Harvard University Press, 1948.

Derrida, Jacques. *A Derrida Reader: Between the Blinds.* Edited by Peggy Kamuf. New York: Columbia University Press, 1991.

Dietrich, Gabriele. "Jüdische-Prophetisches in der modernen deutschen Philosophie und Soziologie." *Horizonte* (Frankfurt am Main) 6 (1971): 375–92.

Eliot, T. S. "Hamlet and His Problems." In *Selected Essays, 1917–1932.* New York: Harcourt, Brace & Co., 1932.

Foerster, Norman, ed. *The Reinterpretation of American Literature: Some Contributions toward the Understanding of Its Historical Development.* New York: Harcourt, Brace & Co., 1928.

Fowler, Roger, ed. *Dictionary of Modern Literary Terms.* London: Routledge and Kegan Paul, 1987.

Friedmann, Friedrich Georg. *Von Cohen zu Benjamin: Zum Problem deutsch-jüdischer Existenz.* Einsiedeln: Johannes Verlag, 1981.

Frye, Northrop. *Anatomy of Criticism: Four Essays.* Princeton: Princeton University Press, 1957.

Garland, Hamlin. *Diaries.* Edited by Donald Pizer. San Marino: Huntington Library, 1968.

Gauss, Christian. *The Papers of Christian Gauss.* Edited by Katherine Gauss Jackson and Hiram Haydn. New York: Random House, 1957.

Geertz, Clifford. "Blurred Genres: The Refiguration of Social Thoughts." *American Scholar* 49 (Spring 1980): 165–66.

Geismar, Maxwell. *Rebels and Ancestors: The American Novel, 1890–1915.* Boston: Houghton Mifflin, 1953.

Genette, Gérard. "Structuralism and Literary Criticism." In *Modern Criticism and Theory,* edited by David Lodge. New York: Longman, 1988.

Glasgow, Ellen. *The Woman Within.* New York: Harcourt, Brace & Co., 1954.

Goethe, Johann Wolfgang von. *Werke in Zwei Bänden.* Edited by Richard Friedenthal. 2 vols. Munich: Droemersche Verlaganstalt, 1953.

Gunn, Giles. *F. O. Matthiessen: The Critical Achievement.* Seattle: University of Washington Press, 1975.

Habermas, Jurgen. *The Philosophical Discourse of Modernity: Twelve Lectures.* Translated by Frederick Lawrence. Cambridge: MIT University Press, 1987.

———. *Philosophical-Political Profiles.* Translated by Frederick G. Lawrence. Cambridge: MIT University Press, 1987.

Hartman, Geoffrey H. *Criticism in the Wilderness: The Study of Literature Today.* New Haven: Yale University Press, 1980.

Heilbut, Anthony. *Exiled in Paradise: German Refugee Artists and Intellectuals in America from the 1930s to the Present.* New York: Viking, 1983.

Heine, Heinrich. *Shakespeare's Mädchen und Frauen.* 1838. Reprint. Frankfurt am Main: Insel Verlag, 1978.

———. *Werke.* Edited by Walther Vontin. Hamburg: Hoffmann und Campe, 1956.

Hirsch, David H. *The Deconstruction of Literature: Criticism after Auschwitz.* Hanover: University Press of New England, 1991.

Horkheimer, Max, and Theodor W. Adorno. *Dialektik der Aufklärung: Philosophische Fragmente.* 1944. Reprint, Frankfurt am Main: Fischer, 1991.

Howard, Jean. "The New Historicism in Renaissance Studies." *English Literary Renaissance* 16 (Winter 1986): 13–43.

Iser, Wolfgang. *The Implied Reader: Patterns of Communication in Prose Fiction from Bunyan to Beckett.* Baltimore: Johns Hopkins University Press, 1974.

Jameson, Frederic. *The Prison-House of Language.* Princeton: Princeton University Press, 1972.

Johnson, Barbara. *The Critical Difference: Essays in the Contemporary Rhetoric of Reading.* Baltimore: Johns Hopkins University Press, 1980.

Kaplan, Alice. *French Lessons.* Chicago: University of Chicago Press, 1993.

Kazin, Alfred. *On Native Grounds: An Interpretation of Modern American Prose Literature.* New York: Reynal and Hitchcock, 1942.

Kermode, Frank. *The Classic: Literary Images of Permanence and Change.* Cambridge: Harvard University Press, 1983.

Korg, James. *Browning and Italy.* Athens: Ohio University Press, 1983.

Kramer, Jane. *Europeans.* New York: Farrar, Straus & Giroux, 1988.

Krupnick, Mark. *Lionel Trilling and the Fate of Cultural Criticism.* Evanston: Northwestern University Press, 1986.

Lehman, David. *Deconstruction and the Fall of Paul de Man.* New York: Poseidon, 1991.

Lerner, Max. *America as a Civilization: Life and Thought in the United States Today.* New York: Simon and Schuster, 1957.

Levine, George, ed. *Speaking for the Humanities.* American Council of Learned Societies, Occasional Paper No. 7. New York: American Council of Learned Societies, 1989.

Lewisohn, Ludwig. *Expression in America.* New York: Harper, 1932.

Lovejoy, Arthur. *The Great Chain of Being.* Cambridge: Harvard University Press, 1936.

Ludwig, Richard M. "Bibliography of the Writings of Howard Mumford Jones to 1963." In *Aspects of American Poetry: Essays Presented to Howard Mumford Jones.* Columbus: Ohio State University Press, 1963.

Lukács, Georg. "The Ideology of Modernism." In *The Critical Tradition,* edited by David H. Richter, 597–611. New York: St. Martin's, 1989.

Lutwack, Leonard. *The Epic Tradition and American Novels of the Twentieth Century.* Carbondale: Southern Illinois University Press, 1971.

———. *The Role of Place in Literature.* Syracuse: Syracuse University Press, 1984.

McCord, David T. W. *Notes on the Harvard Centenary.* Cambridge: Harvard University Press, 1936.

Marx, Leo. *The Machine in the Garden: Technology and the Pastoral Ideal in America.* New York: Oxford University Press, 1964.

Matthiessen, F. O. *American Renaissance: Art and Expression in the Age of Emerson and Whitman.* New York: Oxford University Press, 1941.

Meltzer, Françoise. "Unconscious." In *Critical Terms for Literary Study,* edited by Frank Lentricchia and Thomas McLaughlin. Chicago: University of Chicago Press, 1990.

Morris, Wesley. *Toward a New Historicism.* Princeton: Princeton University Press, 1972.

———. *Friday's Footprint: Structuralism and the Articulated Text.* Columbus: Ohio State University Press, 1979.

Nabokov, Vladimir. *Lectures on Literature.* Edited by Fredson Bowers. New York: Harcourt Brace Jovanovich and Bruccoli Clark, 1980.

———. *Lectures on Russian Literature.* Edited by Fredson Bowers. New York: Harcourt Brace Jovanovich and Bruccoli Clark, 1980.

Naipaul, V. S. *The Enigma of Arrival.* New York: Alfred A. Knopf, 1987.

Nevius, Blake. *Cooper's Landscapes: An Essay on the Picturesque Vision.* Berkeley: University of California Press, 1976.

Nietzsche, Friedrich. *The Portable Nietzsche.* Edited by Walter Kaufmann. New York: Vintage, 1954.

———. *The Use and Abuse of History.* Translated by Adrian Collins. 2d ed. New York: Liberal Arts, 1957.

Novak, Barbara. "On Divers Themes from Nature: A Selection of Texts." In *The Natural Paradise: Painting in America, 1800–1950,* edited by Kynaston McShine, 59–105. New York: Museum of Modern Art, 1976.

Parrington, Vernon Louis. *Main Currents in American Thought: An Interpretation of American Literature from the Beginnings to 1920.* New York: Harcourt, Brace & Co., 1930.

Pearce, Roy Harvey. *Gesta Humanorum: Studies in the Historicist Mode.* Columbia: University of Missouri Press, 1987.

———. *Historicism Once More: Problems and Occasions for the American Scholar.* Princeton: Princeton University Press, 1969.

Peckham, Morse. *The Triumph of Romanticism: Collected Essays.* Columbia: University of South Carolina Press, 1970.

Phillips, J. J., Ishmael Reed, Gundars Strads, and Shawn Wong, eds. *The Before Columbus Foundation Poetry Anthology: Selections from the American Book Awards, 1980–1990.* New York: Norton, 1992.

Ransom, John Crowe. "Introduction." In *Selected Poems of Thomas Hardy,* edited by John Crowe Ransom, ix-xxv. New York: Macmillan, 1961.

Reed, Ishmael, Kathryn Trueblood, and Shawn Wong, eds. *The Before Columbus Foundation Fiction Anthology: Selections from the American Book Awards, 1980–1990.* New York: Norton, 1992.

Remak, Joachim, ed. *The Nazi Years: A Documentary History.* New York: Simon and Schuster, 1969.

Reyes, Alfonso. *The Position of America and Other Essays.* Translated by Harriet de Onis. New York: Alfred A. Knopf, 1950.

Roberts, Julian. *German Philosophy: An Introduction.* Atlantic Highlands, New Jersey: Humanities Press International, 1988.

Rorty, Richard. *Contingency, Irony, and Solidarity.* New York: Cambridge University Press, 1989.

Said, Edward. *Orientalism.* New York: Pantheon, 1978.

Schlegel, Friedrich. *Lucinde and the Fragments.* Edited and translated by Peter Firchow. Minneapolis: University of Minnesota Press, 1971.

Schwab, Arnold T. *James Gibbons Huneker: Critic of the Seven Arts.* Stanford: Stanford University Press, 1963.

Snow, C. P. *Variety of Men.* New York: Scribner's, 1967.

Solomon, Eric. "The Terrible-tempered Mr. Jones." *Harvard Magazine* 80, no. 5 (May/June 1978): 88–90.

Spiller, Robert E. *The Cycle of American Literature: An Essay in Historical Criticism.* New York: Free Press, 1967.

Steel, Ronald. *Walter Lippmann and the American Century.* Boston: Little, Brown & Co., 1980.

Steele, Timothy. *Modern Poetry and the Revolt against Meter.* Fayetteville: University of Arkansas Press, 1990.

Steiner, George. *Extraterritorial: Papers on Literature and the Language Revolution.* New York: Atheneum, 1976.

Stimpson, Catharine. "The Idea of the University." *Partisan Review/2* 58, no. 2 (Spring 1991): 315–49.

Taylor, Charles. *Hegel and Modern Society.* Cambridge: Cambridge University Press, 1979.

Tennenhouse, Leonard. *Power on Display: The Politics of Shakespeare's Genres.* London: Methuen, 1986.

Thomas, Brook. *The New Historicism and Other Old-Fashioned Topics.* Princeton: Princeton University Press, 1991.

Thorslev, Peter L., Jr. *Romantic Contraries: Freedom versus Destiny.* New Haven: Yale University Press, 1984.

Tillyard, E. M. W. *The Epic Strain in the English Novel.* London: Chatto and Windus, 1958.

Todorov, Tzvetan. "Crimes against Humanities." *New Republic* 201, no. 1 (July 3, 1989): 27–29.

Trilling, Lionel. *Beyond Culture: Essays on Literature and Learning.* New York: Harcourt Brace Jovanovich, 1965.

———. *Sincerity and Authenticity.* New York: Harcourt Brace Jovanovich, 1972.

Turner, Frederic Jackson. *The Frontier in American History.* New York: Holt, 1920.

Vanderbilt, Kermit. *American Literature and the Academy: The Roots, Growth, and Maturity of a Profession*. Philadelphia: University of Pennsylvania Press, 1986.

———. *Charles Eliot Norton: Apostle of Culture in a Democracy*. Cambridge: Belknap Press, 1959.

Walcott, Derek. *The Arkansas Testament*. New York: Farrar, Straus & Giroux, 1987.

Wayne, Don E. "The New Historicism." In *Literature and Criticism: A New Century Guide,* edited by M. Kelsall et al. Beckenham, Kent: Croom Helm, 1987.

Wellek, René. "The Content of the Form: Narrative Discourse and Historical Representation, a Review." *Partisan Review*/2 55, no. 2 (Spring 1988): 334–37.

White, Hayden. *Metahistory: The Historical Imagination in Nineteenth-Century Europe*. Baltimore: Johns Hopkins University Press, 1973.

———. *Tropics of Discourse: Essays in Cultural Criticism*. Baltimore: Johns Hopkins University Press, 1978.

Wilson, Edmund. *The Triple Thinkers: Twelve Essays on Literary Subjects*. New York: Oxford University Press, 1948.

Wimsatt, William K, Jr., and Cleanth Brooks. *Literary Criticism: A Short History*. New York: Knopf, 1957.

———. *The Verbal Icon: Studies in the Meaning of Poetry*. Lexington: University of Kentucky Press, 1954.

Index